Manifesting

Your

Best

Life

By

Amanda Rose

© 2018 Amanda Rose

Amanda@AmandaRoseFitness.com

Cover by Daniel McCutcheon

ISBN: *9781726805155*

Dedication

To you, the reader; may this be the guide to making your wildest dreams your reality.

Introduction

LIVE YOUR BEST LIFE

It's a great catch phrase, but what does it mean? Social media is littered with uplifting quotes, many filled with wisdom, and in this digital age we can find ourselves scrolling by and nodding along with them. But what then? We keep scrolling and don't give it a second thought.

We're so caught up in the moment, in the next task, the next day, the next bill to pay, that we don't carve out the time to build the life we really want to live. Most people feel like they are just being swept along in life, like they're just reacting to the circumstances as they come up. But how many consciously create their lives? Not many.

Whether they don't feel like we have enough time, money, energy, opportunities, intelligence, or a slew of other things they tell ourselves they "need," they talk themselves out of even trying. If that sounds familiar, you're not alone. Most people can relate to feeling stuck and have no idea where to turn things around. Well, here's the thing...

Nothing changes if nothing changes. The right time won't just magically appear, the money won't just show up, your schedule isn't slowing down, the opportunities are there, you're smart enough, and anything else you might tell yourself as a reason why you're not living your best life, well, it simply is a way to make yourself feel better about not doing it. I know, I'm calling you out, BUT, if you're reading this, you've already made the first step forward towards CHANGE.

Want to know the secret to living your best life? The answer is so simple that it'll make you go, "OK, but what else?" I know because that's what I asked. I was looking for the magic, secret, hidden answer. In my mind it had to be hard and complicated, it just *had* to be! I mean, otherwise we'd all be living our best life, right?

Well... that ain't so. The big secret? It boils down to knowing exactly what you want, how you want to feel when you get it, staying focused on it, and taking action towards it (no matter how big or small that action might be). I know, I know, it's something we'd call "common sense" or "straight forward." Easy, right?

But most of us, especially in adulthood, aren't thinking ahead about the dream life we want to be living. We're just trying to survive the day, the week, and the month, and keep our head above water while we're at it. Responsibilities come crushing down on us in adulthood; paying rent or a mortgage, car payments, utilities, relationships, raising a family, and working our job(s). It's no wonder most adults set their sights only as far ahead as the next Friday, and that #TGIF is one of the most used hashtags!

The thing most people don't realize, is that every day can feel like Friday when you're living your best life, and that, believe it or not, Monday can be a *really* awesome day of the week. Think I'm crazy? Then you need to keep on reading.

Think back to when you were a kid, with free time, and way fewer responsibilities in life. When your childhood imagination ran wild what did you think about? What did you dream about doing or becoming as a kid? What got you all lit-up inside?

Children don't think about "Why it won't work," they come up with ideas and they pursue them whole-heartedly.

6

Children allow their imaginations to run wild, to allow themselves to dream big. It's a learned behavior to repress our ambitions; through hearing and being told many things like:

"Get your head out of the clouds!"

"Not many people succeed at that."

"What's your back up plan?"

"Be more practical."

"Get a real job!"

"Life isn't a bowl of cherries."

"Are you sure you're good enough to do that?"

All these statements; be it from parents, guardians, teachers, peers, friends, or society, leave us second guessing ourselves, and often walking away from our heart's desires without even trying. The thing is, there are no guarantees in life, it doesn't matter if you pursue your dream job or if you opt for the seemingly 'safe' path. Let's say the safe path is working a desk job at a major company; the company could go under, downsize, a manager might not like you, there's 101 reasons you could lose that job.

So, if there's no certainty, why not pursue what set's your soul on fire? Working a job that you don't like, something that's going to eat up the majority of your waking hours, is soul-crushing. You have just as much opportunity to succeed by pursuing your dream as you do following the 'safe path,' but one is a heck of a lot more fun than the other!

And, with the Law of Attraction at your side, you have the tools to visualize your dream life into reality. If you can see it in your mind, it can show up in your life. The Law of Attraction states that like attracts like. We are all energy, and when we think our brain emits a certain energy, which is then reflected back to us by the Universe. This means one of the most powerful things that you can do is to focus on your dream life in all the detail you can muster. It takes consistency, unshakable faith, and the willingness to follow the signals you receive from the Universe. But, if you're up to the challenge, your dream life awaits you...

IMAGINATION

So, what do you want? Many adults claim they don't know what they want, but the truth is most of us *do* know what we want, it's just scary to say it. Why? Because when we admit what we really want, deep down in our heart of hearts, we feel vulnerable. *What if I go for it and I fail? What will other people think of my dream? What if I'm not good enough to make it?* Our minds drum up all kinds of these fears, and for the vast majority or people, those fears hold them back from even admitting what they really want, let alone to start working towards it.

Without purpose life feels empty and flat. The days drag on, and we wonder why we're even alive when we feel we are without purpose. The thing is, no one else, and no external force can give you purpose. It's something you must decide for yourself.

It may also have been a very long time since you've thought about that burning desire; the flame may now be small, but it's still there. It's time to fan the flames! Find a nice comfortable place to sit, because we are going to work that imagination!

I KNOW WHAT I WANT...

If you already know what you want, even if you've been suppressing it, and haven't admitted that dream to others, then you know what you want. You feel desire, purpose, and passion when you think about what you want. Perhaps fear, feeling that you lacked opportunities, or doubt has held you back from taking action. Today that changes!

You already know what you want, which is the first step. The next step is not shying away from it, not hiding it; you need to focus on it! In as a much detail as you can, you're going to visualize what you want. Picture what a day in your life would look like if you were *living your best life*. How do you wake up? Where do you live? What's your environment look like? What do you do once you get up? Who are you with? What kind of work do you do? How do you feel? Picture everything, down to the small details.

I USED TO KNOW WHAT I WANTED...

If you used to know what you wanted, but that dream no longer resonates with what you want, the great news is you can change it. Perhaps, for example, you used to imagine being the CEO of the company you worked for, but along the way you realized you wouldn't want to have to put in those long hours, and now you're not sure what to do.

What aspects of the position you once coveted made you want it?

What new desires, that conflict with what you once wanted, do you now have?

Chances are your sense of purpose may be tied in with that initial desire, but balancing out your life with what you feel in your heart is important to you is the key is happiness. It's also possible your initial desire is one you felt was imposed by what you felt was expected of you by your parents, your peers, society, etc. If that's the case, wipe that slate clean, and focus in on those new desires. Brainstorm either how to marry-up the best of both, or focus entirely on those new desires and how they can be applied to your life.

I HAVE NO IDEA WHAT I WANT...

If you feel you fall into this category, it's time to do some digging! Let's first narrow things down, ask yourself these following questions:

What brings me joy?

What tasks in my day do I enjoy most?

Do I prefer time alone or being around other people?

Do I prefer being at home or being out in the world?

What do I naturally gravitate to when I have free time?

What makes me excited?

If I had $1,000,000,000.00, after getting the great house/car/dream vacation/etc., what would I do with my time?

These answers will give you a lot of insight into what really matters to you, and open-up a whole bunch of possibilities. The answer to each individual question offers a plethora of options! For example, let's say you prefer being alone, prefer being at home, and in your free time you naturally do a lot of arts and crafts; this suddenly gives us a lot of information about what makes you happy and what you're passionate about! This could translate into opening up your own online arts and crafts shop, fulfilling all of the above desires. It could also mean teaching online courses, through blog, or video, on how to do crafts. Or it could lead to you writing a book about arts and crafts... there are tons of possibilities just based on this little bit of information!

What's the Next Step?

Getting the vision on what your best life looks like is the beginning, but implementing it is where the work really begins. A lot of people dream about the life they want, but it always just stays a buried dream. Life is too damn short to just keep your desires as distant dreams; sitting on your death bed you don't want to look back with regret, thinking about what could have been. As your family and friends sit around you, saying their goodbyes, before you go, as you're about to walk into the white light, you don't want your final thoughts to be, "I wish I'd tried to go for my dreams," with a heavy unfulfilled heart. I know that description is harsh, like the proverbial bucket of ice water thrown in your face, but this is your L I F E and it's too important not to wake you up!

Time keeps ticking, so get to action now, and you'll be living your dream life before you know it. It doesn't matter if your dream feels huge and scary, in fact, it's even better if it does because that means you REALLY want it! And you know what? You can have it. But you have to step up to the plate, and be willing to fail, and fail, and fail, and keep getting back up. The path to success is paved with countless failures; if you're not failing, you're not doing anything very innovative. That means you're going to have to face some fears, pull up your big boy/girl pants, and get in it for the long haul.

Yes, the journey down this path is the one less travelled. It's the one that will push you out of your comfort zone and force you to grow. It's also the path that has unspeakable joys. The best part? You're not alone, the Universe has your back. And when you make big leaps to grow as a person, you'll meet other people who are doing the same, and you will lift each other up!

The only question is... are you ready?

WHAT TO EXPECT:

- Work on getting clear about what you really want, so you know exactly what you best life looks like
- Put into action new supportive habits that will move you towards your goals
- Learn how the Law of Attraction supports or hinders all your endeavors, based on your

thoughts, and how to get them in support mode all of the time

- Instilling daily habits to put you in sync with attracting what you really want
- Living your best life!

What You'll need:

- Set aside approximately 30 minutes a day to read through, and, practice each day's lesson.
- Get a journal, or set up a word document on your computer, to go through this book's activites. The big life changing work we're about to embark on will require you to, well... do the work! This process is fun and exciting, but you'll need to track your thoughts and progress to get the most out of it.

For some people writing things down takes them out of the moment, disconnecting them from their emotions, and feelings are an important aspect of manifestation. If you wish to write during the course but notice you're in your head thinking more than feeling when you write, simply finish writing the lesson out, then review what you've wrote, and get back into your body and your heart with those thoughts.

Chapter 1: Clarity

We began to look at what you really want for your life in the introduction. Now it's time to dig in, and get really clear on those things. Having clarity about what we want allows the Universe to step in and help us. The Law of Attraction works based on energy; everything in the Universe is energy, and like attracts like. When you have a thought, your brain emits energy, and that gets reflected back to you. The Universe immediately begins to move things into motion to make that thought a reality in the physical world, however the speed is not instantaneous in seeing the results.

That is why clarity on what you want is so important, you have to keep focused on it. If you think, "I want to be a full-time artist," and then think, "Oh but that's not realistic, it's too hard to stand out," the second thought is cancelling out the first. Fear and doubt are natural, we simply have to be aware of those negative defeating thoughts when they arise and replace them with our main focus.

Uncertainty, constantly changing the direction of our thinking, sends mixed signals, and then constantly interrupts the energetic flow. If you have real clarity about what you want, it's much easier to redirect your thoughts to that vision of your life. Without that clarity, you'll be left wondering, "is this what I really want?" and be stuck in a loop of going nowhere.

You're starting to get a basic idea of what living your best life will look like, now let's expand on it. Grab your journal, it's time to brainstorm! On your paper write the following headings, and leave about 5 lines, or a couple inches, beneath each heading:

LOVE

HEALTH

FINANCE

CAREER

FAMILY

FRIENDS

HOBBIES AND LEISURE

TRAVEL

HOME

OTHER

Now that you have your headings, the real work begins. Living your best life is about balance; happiness doesn't come from success or achievement all in one area of your life. What good is a great career if your home life falls apart? A lot of people feel you need choose, that you can have one or the other. That's a load of crap! You can have both.

Your job here is to go through each one of these categories and, in your own way, jot down your perfect version of each area in your life. You might point form ideas that makes sense to you, or you might need to explain it in detailed paragraphs; the key is that you think it through and express those thoughts in ways the will summon up these thoughts in the future.

As you go through each heading ask yourself these questions:

"When I'm Living my Best Life..."

- What's this part of my life look like?
- What brings me happiness about this?
- How does it make me feel?

- What aspects of this do I see in my day to day life?

- Who (if anyone) am I with?

- Where am I?

Asking these questions will help you to think through what it will actually be like to live it and help you to be sure you're saying what you really want. These answers should make you feel exhilarated! With excitement it's natural to feel some fear, and the fear comes from not knowing the 'how'. You don't need to know the how, just focus on this work. The one thing you want to make sure isn't happening is any feelings of suppression.

Let's say for example you're picturing your dream home and you're imagining a big beautiful old fashioned Victorian home, but deep down you know you'd prefer a modern house on the beach, you know the beach home is the right answer. Sometimes we lie to ourselves about what we want, because other people wanted it for us. Often parents, teachers, or people we looked to as mentors, impart their dream for us, but it's not necessarily the dream we have for ourselves. At the end of the day you're the one that has to live your life, so set your sights on what YOU want; that's all that really matters.

It's also important you don't cancel out possibilities. Let's say, for example, you're working on the HEALTH area of your life, and you suffer from chronic arthritis. Don't resign yourself here as indefinitely suffering from arthritis, and put something wimpy down like, "I want to have less pain," because that statement means you expect to always live in pain. And what do we know about the Law of Attraction? You get what you ask for! So, make it a bold, "When I'm living my best life I'm pain free!"

Let your heart lead you, and your imagination run without boundaries. In life we are the only ones who truly get in the way of actualizing our own dreams. So, get out of the way, and let your inner most want's and desires come out, and onto the page. No editorializing, no judging, no doubting, no logical rationalizing; this is your time to say what you want, LOUD AND PROUD!

The OTHER category is entirely up to you. You may or may not choose to use it, based on if your want's and desires all fit into the main categories. However, for example, perhaps Charity Work is incredibly important to you, and something you have always wanted to be very active in, or even something you'd want to start your own organization for. You may choose to make something like that its own category, so you can envision how that project would work and all the lives it would impact.

As you go through each area of your life, take a moment to close your eyes and really imagine living it. If it's in alignment with what you really want, it'll make you feel happy and excited. Follow that feeling! Now get writing!

To-Do List

- Write out categories above and leave space to write beneath them
- Picture what each area of my life looks like when you're Living your Best Life
- Answer questions above for each category to help gain perspective about what you really want

Chapter 2: Top 10 Goals List

Grab your work from the Clarity practice, because now we're going to make some choices, hone in on some specifics, and move mountains! You've heard the saying before, "A goal without a deadline is a just a dream." If you're going to move into the realm of living your best life, we must anchor those dreams in the real world, and the only way to do that is to set deadlines!

As soon as you have a deadline, it forces you to take action. When you know what you want (*clarity and focus*) and you start to move towards it (*take action*) then the Universe will start to move things into place to support you. Action is the bridge between thought & energy, and the physical world, making it a major key in the manifestation process.

Looking over all of the things you wrote down, across all areas of your life, you are going to pick the 10 of them. The ones that you pick should ones that would blow your hair back, and knock your socks off, if they happened within the next year, because they would radically change your life for the better! Looking over it all, what would be scary, yet crazy cool, if you accomplished them in the next 12 months? Be brave here, don't just choose things you know are already going to happen. For example, you wouldn't put down "I'll own my car free and clear," if you know your car payments are done this year anyways. Also, we're not worrying about the 'how' yet, so again, no censoring the list!

When you write out this list, do so in "I" statements, as if they're already accomplished. This turns them into affirmations, and affirmations help us to focus our mind on what we want, and see the end result we're aiming to manifest. Visualization is a big part of manifestation, so utilizing it in this fashion is increasingly helpful. It also helps you to wipe out doubt, by not using phrasing like, "I hope _____ happens this year." Or "If _____ happens it'll be amazing!" You're eliminating the possibility of it not happening and taking ownership of your life!

Write today's date at the top of this list, so you can come back to it at any time and see your progressing along your 12-month time line. Don't worry about writing them in any particular order, we're going to figure out what to start with once you've got your list done. Ready? Set? Go!

READ THROUGH YOUR LIST

After you've got your top 10 goal list for the next 12 months, read through it, and picture each one being accomplished. After you read each one, say "Thank you!" to the Universe, as if it's already been achieved! Gratitude is the fastest way to actualize our goals; when we're grateful we feel happy, and that's a strong vibrational energy sent out to the Universe to be reflected back to us. So, when you look at, read through, or visualize your goals, always follow it up with a big, "Thank you!"

DOMINO EFFECT

The domino effect is when one event sets off a chain of events. We're going to apply to domino effect to you list! When you're reviewing your list, we need to choose one of those 10 goals to start working on first, and we want it to be the goal that helps several or all of your other goals to fall into place. For example, let's say this is your list for the next 12 months:

1. I am travelling to the Maldives for a Vacation
2. I am the CEO of a successful cupcake store
3. I have paid off my mortgage

4. I am debt free
5. I have girls' night every week with my best friends
6. I got married to the love of my life
7. I have learned to speak Spanish
8. I founded a charity to help animals
9. I live in my dream home, in Arizona overlooking a canyon
10. I have more vitality than I did as a teenager

So, when we look over our list we want to think, "If I achieve this goal, which other goals, if any, fall into place?" For the example above, #2 has the potential to make 1, 3, 4, 8, and 9 happen. By focusing in on the creating the successful business, the financial offspring from that aids in accomplishing all of the goals that require money.

It's important to remember to the not so obvious effects as well. For example, perhaps in getting your cupcake shop super successful, you end up turning it into a franchise, and that franchise might end up going into multiple countries, including Spanish speaking countries, prompting your need to learn Spanish into full gear as part of your work day. Or, perhaps, as you set things up to run your store, the guy who you buy the ingredients asks you out, you hit it off, and that's the guy you marry! The key thing here, is in focusing on these top 10 goals, and working towards them, they fall into place in ways you never imagined!

Looking over your own list, think through each item on there and how accomplishing it will help any of the others come to fruition, in part or in full. Once you've determined the goal that will cause the domino effect on your list, place a star next to it to mark it as the first goal you'll work towards.

To-Do List

- Write out your top 10 goals list using the "I" statement format
- Determine the goal that will have a domino effect on your list, and place a star next to it to mark it as your first goal to work on

Chapter 3: Action

If you flipped ahead, you've seen that PLAN is the next chapter heading, and you might wonder why we're looking at *action* before we look at planning! No, it's not an accident. There's an important reason action comes first!

One of the biggest stumbling blocks people run into in life is not taking action! Why? Mostly because of fear. Fear of failure, fear of success, fear of making a mistake, fear of being judged – you name it! So, all too often, people like to sit in the thought/dream/plan part of things. Unfortunately, that won't ever bring your dreams to fruition. If you want to move forward, you have to take action!

"But if I don't plan, how will I know what action to take?" you're probably asking. Here's the thing, you're going to plan... but as you go! This way you aren't allowed to sit indefinitely in the planning stage, you've decided what you want, you're going to start moving towards it, and you're going to adjust course en route. This is what successful people do, and that's why this is the way you're going to do it too!

The initial action you're going to take is going to be *intuitive action*. Intuitive action is when you act based on a feeling or nudge that it's the right thing to do; you don't necessarily know why, and it may not even seem like it has anything do to with your goal. It's important not to fight this, or pre-judge it, just go with the flow.

What happens when you decide on what you want, you start to think about and visualize it, is that you're communicating those desires to the Universe. The Universe is then able to start pushing you and your goal towards each other. This is the big reason why we don't not need to know the 'how'; we'll be shown the how. This is particularly hard if you're the kind of person, who, erm... maybe is a control freak? Perfectionist? I get it. I used to be both. There's nothing wrong with being detail oriented, but when we decide that we have to have absolute control of every minute detail, then we can stand in the way of other better possibilities that were beyond our realm of comprehension at the time.

If you consider yourself to be a perfectionist or a control freak, use this as a way to grow and learn from another approach. If there's one thing I've learned from letting go of my need to control, it's that life can be more fun, AND I can get more done too. Your meticulous skills will still come in handy in shaping the work once it's underway.

TAKING INTUITIVE ACTIVE

To take intuitive, the first thing you want to do is get into communication with the Universe, so you can be directed. The easiest way to do this is to visualize your goal and be grateful for it as if it's already been achieved. Let's get started!

1. Find a quiet place to sit where you won't be interrupted.

2. Close your eyes and focus on your breathing. Release any tension you may be holding onto in your body. Sit as long as you need until you feel relaxed and at peace.

3. Thinking of your #1 goal (AKA domino goal) from your top 10 goal list, picture the moment that goal comes to full fruition, and visualize the entire experience...

    a. How do you find out the news that it's been achieved?

    b. Where are you?

    c. How do you feel?

    d. What do you sense (taste, touch, see, smell, hear)?

    e. Who are you with?

    f. Who is the first person you share the good news with?

    g. How will you celebrate?

4. Take a moment to say thank you as if it's already happened.

5. Affirm the goal with your "I" statement for the goal.

6. Open your eyes.

You've just put a lot of energy into focusing on your goal, and as we know the Law of Attraction is all about our energy vibration being reflected back to us. The Universe is already underway to send back what you've pictured into the physical world. Think about bringing that dream into reality; what's your first impulse? Go do that now! No waiting, no judging, no hesitating, just go!

Every journey starts with a single step, and the biggest things in life are accomplished bit by bit, inch by inch. So, maybe your impulse was to go online and research, maybe you felt the need to go take a walk or a drive, maybe you suddenly thought of someone who'd want to do it with you and you're calling them up on the phone; the thing is you're in motion taking action! Now you're on the playing field, and, we can see the cues and course correct.

"A BODY IN MOTION TENDS TO STAY IN MOTION."

-ISAAC NEWTON

Remember physics class? Once you're in motion you tend to stay in motion. The hardest thing... getting into motion! So, that's what we're doing first, because getting started is the number one thing people put off. Staying in motion is the easy part comparably!

SEE WHERE IT TAKES YOU

Once you're in motion, things begin to fall into place; awareness is your biggest asset now. Pay attention to what opportunities are coming up to take you to the second step. Keep focused on your end game. Now that you're in motion, we're going to apply planning.

To-Do List

- Read through your top 10 list
- Go through the Taking Intuitive Action Practice
- Take Intuitive Action on your #1 Goal!

Chapter 4: Plan

Now we're ready to start applying some planning to your domino goal. When you take the Law of Attraction, a solid goal, and sprinkle in some planning and discipline... magic happens! You're already in action, which means you're starting to get your bearings in regard to achieving your goal. Perhaps by taking intuitive action you've learned something new, have a better understanding what it's going to take to reach it, feel more motivated, met someone who can help you; whatever the case, you're on the road, and now we must take the wheel and steer!

So, what's the best way to be successful in the endeavor you've chosen? What should your plan be? You don't just want to plan for planning's sake, you want it to be effective!

DON'T RECREATE THE WHEEL

The best way to come up with an effective action *plan* is to take a look at what successful people in your field of pursuit did to get where they are. Even if you're doing something new that hasn't exactly been done before, you can look at what other tend-setters and way-pavers did in order to make their dream into a reality. It's important to remember that someone even in a completely different field whose been extremely successful has impeccable habits you can learn from.

Research someone in your desired field and learn what they did to overcome the odds. How did they start? What daily habits did they implement? How many times did they have to fail before they succeeded? What obstacles did they face? What did they do to stay motivated? Who did they rely on? Get as educated as possible on their journey to gain insight into what worked!

CONSISTENCY

Commit to being consistent. One of the most useful tools in your toolbox is using momentum to propel you forward. Think of a train; when a train starts up it's slow and takes a lot of effort just to creep along the track. That speed slowly picks up until the train is zooming along, with so much force, it can bulldoze through a car sitting in its way! You want to use that momentum to your advantage.

If you're constantly starting and stopping, you're wasting the biggest percentage of your energy to just "get back in the flow," so don't get out of the flow! Now, I'm not suggestion that you become a work-a-holic, what I *AM* suggesting is that your goal gets some daily attention. Your goal is too important to leave to chance, you must schedule time for it.

DAILY MINIMUMS

Boil down what needs to be done to reach your goal into daily minimums. These minimums are tasks you will accomplish on even your crazy-busiest days. That means these daily targets have to be the most important things to do towards achieving your goal. Figure out what the most important things you need do to are, and then create a to-do list you can use daily to check these activities off as you accomplish them.

BRIGHT AND EARLY

I'm a big fan of making the most important things you want to do each day the *first* things you do each day. In the morning, you're fresh... well, some of us need coffee first, but aside from procaffeinating, the morning is the best time to get things done. For one, the tasks will get done and be out of the way early in your day, so you don't have to worry about doing them all day long – the stress relief *alone* is worth that! You will be able to be more focused on the other needs of your day when you don't have that lingering "I need to get that done later," thought hovering at the back of your mind.

You get to accomplish something right at the start of your day, this gives you positive neural feedback. It's been shown when people check things off their to-do list that the brain releases dopamine AKA the feel good neuroreceptor! This little brain hack can get you hooked on success!

Most importantly, it will *actually* get done. The biggest problem with leaving things to the end of the day, is they tend to get shoved to *tomorrow,* and then? Tomorrow never comes. At the end of the day we're mentally and physically tired, and its way more appealing to curl up on the couch with a bowl of popcorn than it is to work on a goal.

Look at your schedule, when do you normally get up? Set your alarm 30-60 minutes earlier and use that time to take steps toward your goal. Before you complain that you're not an early bird, neither am I. DO IT ANYWAY! You'll adapt, and the best things in life take some effort!

MOTIVATION

Having a solid motivating reason behind your goal is going to be the defining factor between you reaching it or giving up. There will be days where you will not want to do anything, and on those days, you need a strong reason to see you through. You had to dig deep when you made that goals list, so they must mean something to you! So, your job is to clearly know that *why* behind your goal, so you can remind yourself that the goal is bigger than how you happen to feel in the moment.

To-Do List

- Determine what successful people in your field (or similar field) have done and write down what those habits are
- Write out your daily must-do minimums habits
- Set your alarm to go off 30-60 minutes earlier so you have daily time to work on your goals; this is the time you'll do you daily must-do minimums
- Write out *why* you have to accomplish this goal!

Chapter 5: Failure

Uh-oh…. The *F* word. Failure. Just the idea of failure has stopped enumerable dreams before they even got to see the light of day. For some reason, somewhere along the way, failure became unacceptable. The irony? Failure is the road to success.

Get comfortable with being uncomfortable, because you are going to fail. If you are going to pursue your best life, live big, large, and in charge, then honey, get ready to fail. It's a necessary part of the journey, and it's time to stop seeing it as a *bad* thing!

Do you ever read or watch celebrity success stories? Or business success stories? Or inventor success stories? Or… well, any success stories? Biographies, documentaries, heck even those 2-3-minute social media videos floating around summarizing peoples' accomplishments, the information is readily out there and in our faces about how others succeeded in their field. We tend to look at people who have already "made it" and for some reason just want to assume it was easy for them; but the path to success is littered in struggle and failure.

Think about the great authors, such as Stephen King (Carrie), J.K. Rowling (Harry Potter), and Margaret Mitchell (Gone with the Wind), who were rejected countless times by publishers. Or consider Thomas A. Edison who failed 1000 times before creating the light bulb. Or look at Sylvester Stallone in the 1970's, who, when he'd written the script for the film Rocky, was so broke he had to sell his dog to make sure his dog would go to a family where he knew he'd be fed, was offered several hundred thousand dollars for his script with the condition Stallone wouldn't be in it... and he turned them down, and so they turned him down. We all know these names as being wildly successful, but the journey wasn't a straight line, it wasn't obvious they would succeed.

HINDSIGHT IS 20/20

It all looks crystal-clear when it's over, and we're looking back at it. In the moment, when the future is uncertain, it's not so easy to be confident in the outcome. Failure along the way may make you question your resolve. This is why you HAVE to remember this:

YOU ONLY TRULY FAIL IF YOU QUIT.

Rejection and failure along the path, that's how you grow, that's how you test your willpower, that's how you get BETTER! If success was a straight line, then everybody would be following their dreams. It's not, and that, quite frankly, scares most people to death. They'd rather play it safe than risk failure; but you know what happens when you don't try? *If you don't try then you have **already failed.***

Ouch! Right? The idea of that should hurt because you are trying to break free of living a *less than* life. There's nothing more tragic than someone laying in their deathbed and feeling regret about all of the things that they never did. Don't let that even be a glimmer of a possibility for you.

CHANGE YOUR PERSPECTIVE ABOUT FAILING

Failing is part of the process, so embrace it! When you try new things, you're going to hit road bumps. Just don't give up! Learn from those bumps on the road, they teach you what's not working so you can figure out what does work!

To-Do List

- Read a biography, or watch a documentary or interview, on someone who has achieved something great. Pay attention to all the pitfalls they had to go through on their journey. Imagine being in their shoes, not knowing or having any guarantees of success ahead, experiencing the failures they went through. See that they're not super human, they just never gave up. Implement the affirmation, "If they can do it, so can I!"

- On a piece of paper write "I WILL NOT GIVE UP!" and pin up that piece of paper in the space you're working on your goals where you'll see it as a daily reminder.

Chapter 6: Gratitude

The surest way to ensure your goals become part of your reality is to focus on being grateful for them, as if they've already happened. Gratitude is the gateway to manifesting what you want. In the introduction we talked about how visualizing was the key to achieving your goals, now we're going to dive into why...

EVERYTHING IS ENERGY

You, me, the sun, the stars – the whole Universe is all energy. Every kind of energy is vibrating at its own certain frequency, and like attracts like. This is the basic principle known as the Law of Attraction. The frequency you're vibrating at is dictating exactly what you're attracting into your life.

The great thing about this, as you can see, is that the concept is really simple! You simply need to get into alignment with what you want in order to be able to draw it into your life. The hard part? Your subconscious is in control, not your conscious mind.

You must first get to the root of your beliefs, which are dictated by your subconscious mind. It kind of works like this in regard to your subconscious vs your conscious mind: you open your fridge and there's this nasty stank that smacks you in the face, so you put a baking soda air freshener in the fridge. The next day, you open the fridge, and bam, that stank is still there, even though you put the air freshener in there. The smell is still lingering because you didn't get rid of the massive rotting tomato that's sitting in the crisper liquifying into a putrid mess. The subconscious (rotting tomato) can't be fixed by the conscious effort (baking soda air freshener). You have to get rid of the subconscious belief that's sabotaging you in order to get rid of that gross, nauseating, make-you-weak-in-the-knees smell.

If you've read *Manifesting on Purpose: A 3 Week Guide to Transforming Your Life Through the Law of Attraction,* then you already have a solid idea about how this all works. Pull out that book again and go through the practices to ensure you're maintaining daily gratitude practices. If you haven't read it, go get it, the in-depth work on changing your sub-conscious beliefs is imperative to living your best life.

The best way to see what those deep-down beliefs are, since they often aren't apparent to us, is to take a look at all the areas in your life and see which ones you're struggling in. Those areas are screaming, "Hey, unsupportive belief livin' here!" So, on a scale of 1 to 10, 1 being the absolute worst-case scenario, and 10 being that you're already living your best life in that area of your life, rate yourself in each of these categories:

Love

Money

Career

Relationships

Family

Travel

Friends

Health

Happiness

Projects

Maybe you scored a 10 on your love life, but your finances are sitting at a 2; then it's a good chance you've got some very unsupportive beliefs about money! Anything you scored yourself as having a 7 or less on, investigate. Ask yourself:

- What were my parents beliefs about _____?
- Did any particular event happen that made an impression on me about _____?
- As I was growing up, what did I notice the media and societies view was on _____?
- How did my teachers and mentors feel about _____?

Try to find the root of that belief. Once you know why you think the way you do, it's much easier to release those beliefs. When you're born you're a blank slate, you don't know what to believe, and you learn what to believe from the people around you. No belief is inherently right or wrong, they are merely supportive or unsupportive of who you want to be and what you want to do with your life. Now that you're an adult and have awareness, you can choose what you want to believe.

As you uncover the foundation of each unsupportive belief, release it:

"I no longer find believing that _____ supports who I want to be, so I am choosing to let it go!"

And then, replace the old beliefs with new supportive ones. If you're struggling with money and your old subconscious motto was, "If I have money I can't be loved!" because as a kid you always saw your parents fighting about money, you can now objectively replace that belief with something like, "I can have money AND love!" As an objective adult you know that even if your parents fought about money, that money isn't inherently good or bad. Money is a means to be and do more of what you already are and do; it doesn't have wants and needs of its own.

EGO, ♪AHHH FREAK OUT♫!

As you move through shaking your foundational beliefs, get ready for the ego to start throwing a temper tantrum, the likes of which you've never seen. The ego is that insecure, sacred, sometimes showing-off-too-much for attention/love/approval from others, part of ourselves. The ego wants to be safe, and secure, and to keep things normal and predictable, and... boring!

The ego fears the unknown, so when you're embarking on building your dream life, to live you best life, that's... outside of your comfort zone, and the ego will FREAK OUT. It's important to be aware of this so you don't allow the ego to scare you back into submission. What's scarier, breaking through your fear to live the most amazing life you've ever imagined, or living a mediocre life? Yeah, I thought so. Time to break through...

So, what's going to happen? The ego will bring on challenges, mini-freak-outs, and manifest situations that will make you ask, "Am I doing the right thing?" Maybe you start a new business and the water main breaks and floods your new space, or your business partner backs out, or you get in a car accident on the way to an important meeting, or your merchandise order of 1000 "Hello" bears arrive as "Hell" bears; the point is, you're always manifesting, and the fear based ego will attract some crazy things while it's freaking out about the change to try and scare you into quitting.

First of all, yes, you're doing the right thing. Anyone whose done anything amazing and worth doing has had to go through this painful stint of growth. Your faith and commitment will be tested to the max. The Universe wants to know just how serious you are! Don't let your ego deter you from going after your hearts desires. As you grow through these events, whatever they may be for you, then you will expand your comfort zone.

THANK YOU

Coming back around to gratitude; your thankful heart will see you through all the changes, and keep you focused on where you're headed. At the end of the day, if we're still alive and breathing, you bet there are things to be grateful for! Gratitude puts you at the helm for manifesting and knocks ego out of the driver's seat.

You can't feel grateful and feel fear/doubt/depression simultaneously. Gratitude is the easiest way to feel happiness in an instant, it gets our minds to seek out the good, and since like attracts like, we want to be focused on the good! We're going to make gratitude a habit!

THE GRATITUDE MINUTE

If there's one thing we need when life's busy, it's reminders. Until we've firmly ingrained a new habit in our daily routine, getting a prompt is the best way to make sure it happens. You can set a reminder on your computer or phone to prompt you with a notification. Have it go off 3 times a day, and name it "Gratitude Minute."

When the reminder pops up, set a timer for one minute, and during that minute close your eyes and think about what you're grateful for. You can be grateful for a myriad of things; what's happened in your day so far, your health, family, love, money, work, the air in your lungs, a beautiful image you saw earlier, the fact that you have a minute to just sit and breathe, your senses, indoor plumbing, cheese; literally whatever comes to mind that you're thankful about! Big, small, it doesn't matter. What matters is that it brings you joy, and you're happy you have it in your life experience.

You're going to feel so refreshed after that minute, that you'll be more efficient afterward. You'll be a better problem solver, because your mind will be tuned into looking for the good, you'll see past any issues you may face.

You'll feel happier, less stressed, be much more present in the moment, and you'll kick more ass.

To-Do List

- Remember that everything is energy, and the frequency you're vibrating at is what you're attracting back
- Figure out what beliefs are not supporting you in who you want to become, let them go, and replace them with new supportive beliefs
- Set up your Gratitude Minute reminders in your phone or on your computer

Chapter 7:

Vibrational Alignment

One of the things that begins to happen when you intentionally practice the Law of Attraction daily is unexpected blessings! Good things just start happening. It's like you suddenly got 'luckier' but luck has nothing to do with it; the Universe is simply reflecting your high vibrations back to you! Let me give you an example...

BLESSINGS OUT OF THE BLUE!

The other day I was visiting a friend who lives on the other side of the city, and on my way home I stopped by a grocery store I don't normally shop at. I got what I needed and was at the cash. I was trying to pay with my VISA, while the cashier wasn't paying attention and chatting to a co-worker I kept getting a card error.

Finally, the cashier clues in and asks if I'm using a VISA, I say yes, and she tells me they don't accept it. I ask if they take American express and she says yes, so I try that card. Again errors. I apologize to the line up behind me, as now I've been trying several minutes to struggle to pay. The cashier then asks her co-worker if they accept American Express; they don't.

My only other card on me is my debit, and I couldn't use it because it's linked up to my old checking account, which now doesn't exist. I'm standing there, not sure what to do, but I didn't want to have to leave without my groceries after spending all that time shopping. I had a busy week ahead, and no other time to go out to re-shop.

Then, out of the blue, the lady behind me says, "If you don't have any way to pay I can pay for you." I just looked at her for a moment, shocked by the kind offer. I tell her she doesn't need to do that, but she smiles warmly and tells me she's happy to. Having no other way to pay, I accept her offer and thank her profusely. I tell her I will pay it forward the next time I see someone in need.

That act of kindness was a true blessing in my day. I kept replaying the situation in my mind thinking, "Thank you, thank you, thank you!" and setting my intention to bless that woman for her generosity.

The Universe works through us. Make sure your vibration is set high on receiving; you never know how things will come to you! Abundance can come by way of a discount, a coupon, something being lent to you so you don't have to buy it, a gift, something you find, or even a complete stranger buying your groceries for you!

BEING A GOOD RECEIVER

Have you ever tried to give someone a gift, and they didn't appreciate it, or were all awkward about it? That feels awful as the giver. When we get a gift for someone we get all excited, imagine their excitement and joy when they'll open it; a lot of thought and love goes into it! All that wonderful energy bottoms out when the person doesn't receive it well.

If you act all icky and weird when you get things, why would anyone want to get you anything? That includes the Universe; the energy you send out gets reciprocated. If you're all uncomfortable about getting stuff, the Universe will say, "OK, you don't like receiving, so don't worry, not sending you anything."

Giving and receiving are OPPOSITES and EQUALS. We live on a planet of duality; one is meaningless without the other. One isn't better or worse than the other; you can't give if there's no one to receive, and you can't get if there's no one to give! So, if you've always preferred to be a giver, take a moment to realize that if you're not tickle-pink when you receive, you're robbing other givers of the joy of giving!

START PRACTICING

Giving and receiving isn't always physical. Compliments are one way we give and receive on a regular daily basis. This is an excellent way to begin practicing receiving without being weird about it! It will also really increase your awareness, you're going to start seeing just how often people do not receive well!

It's alarmingly common that when someone gets a compliment they deflect it or down play it!

EXAMPLE 1

Down playing:

GIVER "Thanks for your help on the bi-annual reports."

RECEIVER "Oh, it was nothing."

Accepting:

GIVER "Thanks for your help on the bi-annual reports."

RECEIVER "You're welcome!"

EXAMPLE 2

Deflecting:

GIVER "You look great!"

RECEIVER "I Look like crap!"

Accepting:

GIVER "You look great!"

RECEIVER "Thank you!"

To make things easy, *Thank You* and *You're Welcome* are the 2 phrases you need to keep handy moving forward. These statements acknowledge and accept what you're being given. You'll empower yourself, and you'll make the giver feel good about their compliment! It's a win-win!

WELCOME THE BOUNTY

Open yourself up to more opportunities to receive! The simplest way to do this is to let the Universe know you are ready to receive. Add it to your daily affirmations: *"Universe, I am ready and willing to receive any and all of your blessings! Thank you, thank you, thank you!"*

To-Do List

- Get clear about Giving and Receiving being opposite but equal
- Practice Receiving
- Ask the Universe for more opportunities to receive

Chapter 8: Fear

"Fear kills more dreams then failure ever will!" *Write. That. Down!* Put that up in your work space, make it a reminder in your phone; you need to know that feeling fear is normal, and even the most successful people feel the fear. The difference between success and struggle? Letting the fear stop you OR feeling the fear and doing what you need to do anyways!

We have this incredible imagination, that has this ability to run off on tangents. In our minds we've lived through countless incredible tragedies about what *could happen*. It's these fears that often hold people back from taking action, and if you never try, you've already failed.

FEAR RESPONSE

Fearing the unknown is our natural response. It's instinctual when faced with a new situation that our fear kicks in. While this response feels very unhelpful in our modern lives, it's what's kept us alive as a species.

When we were living in caves, hunting and gathering our food, and, you know, just trying to survive, having a healthy fear of the unknown was what kept from getting eaten alive. Human beings aren't particularly good predators, we rely on our intelligence to survive. Awareness of our surrounding, and caution, meant we could go out and explore and very likely come back to tell the tale. This fear response is still very much a part of who we are now.

FEARLESS IS A LIE

Don't expect to suddenly become fearless. If you wait for the fear to pass in order to take action, you're going to be waiting... forever! When we look at successful people we often see them as being fearless, but that's a misconception. It's still buckle-in-the-knees scary for them to try new things and push boundaries, they just do it anyways. And that's what we need to do as well! Feel the fear but do what we need to do anyways!

The good news? It's only scary when it's new, after that, you know what to expect and it's no longer terrifying! The bad news? Every new thing we do is going to be scary. Knowing this, you're armed to succeed. You just have to breathe through the scary part! After that initial terror passes, the great thing is, you discover the joy and triumphs!

You move past your own self-imposed limitations and you get to experience whole new levels of awesomeness!

Think back to the first time you tried something new, like, for example, riding a rollercoaster. It's scary as hell, but it's also exciting, so you use your excitement to push through the fear as you're waiting in line for your turn. You think about maybe getting out of line, but you push through it, and stay the course. Then it's your turn to get into the coaster, your heart starts racing, adrenaline pumping, as you climb into the seat and get your safety harness buckled up.

As you're waiting for all the other passengers to get in and ready you start doubting your choices. *What the hell am I doing here?! What if my harness fails and I fall right out of my seat on that upside-down loopy thing? Oh my god, what if this thing wasn't built right and it flies right off of the rails?!* Fear and panic are setting in and your mind is creating a ton of wild stories. You're about to call over the attendant, when, it's too late... the ride has begun.

You're at the point of no return, the coaster is moving slowly at first, creeping up, up, up, to the top of the first peak. You start to think, *OK, this isn't so bad,* but then, you crest the peak. Suddenly the coaster plunges at an alarming speed, your hair is *whooshing* behind you and you're screaming your head off. But you're not screaming because you're scared, you're screaming because it's exhilarating!

You realize your harness is holding, the coaster isn't flying off the tracks, and *Oh my god, here comes the upside-down loop!* And you zoom around and watch the world turn, and suddenly you are right side up again and it was *amazing!* All too fast the ride comes to an end, and all you can think about it getting back in line for another turn!

Things that terrify us at first can often become our favorite things in life. You have to push past the fear to give them a chance. Fear and excitement have similar energy to them, having a combination of both when approaching a new situation is normal, so try to lean into the excitement as a way to push past the fear!

Feel the fear and do it anyways!

To-Do List

- Remember that Fear is a natural response
- Look at someone successful you admire and acknowledge what it must have felt like for them before they found success, and the fears they had to face to get to where they are now
- Remind yourself of a time you were afraid of something, but after you did it, you felt amazing and liberated
- Commit to acting in spite of fear

Chapter 9: Circle of 5

I have to admit, years and years ago, the first time I read about how, "You are the sum of the 5 people you're closest to," that I rolled my eyes. I hated the idea of being influenced. I was convinced this didn't apply to me, that I was in control, and that the people around me didn't impact me. Until... I did the exercise. I followed what the book said, of course determined I'd prove it wrong, and instead I got proven wrong. The theory was right. I *was* the sum of the 5 people I spent the most time with. *Uh-oh!*

This was one of those hard wake-up call moments for me. As easy as it would be to say, "You know what, just gonna skip this chapter..." I didn't. I decided to dive in further and learn more, because clearly, this was a weak area in my life. As an introvert, I didn't socialize much, and a lot of my relationships were really old ones with people that... weren't really ambitious.

Now, I also spent a lot of time with go-getter people I worked with, who had positive attitudes and big dreams. So, between my 5 people, I landed, you guessed it, right in the middle. I was ambitious, I had big dreams, and big goals, but

I also had some of the bad habits of my less ambitious friends.

Like most people the big fear I had was having to get rid of my friends in order to pursue the person I wanted to become. So, what I'm going to tell you now if that's the fear you're feeling is, don't worry. We're going to talk about that, and no, you don't have to go tell the people who aren't necessarily helping you to take a hike.

THE SUM OF 5

One of the easiest measures to do this circle of 5 exercise with is finances. Money is a direct indicator of the results we're producing. Of course, there are times in life when you're on the right track, but finances aren't booming, say at the beginning of a new business venture, however we're talking overall here. Maybe you don't know exact figures of the 5 people you spend the most time with, but you can see the lifestyle they live; you're trying to look at where the 5 people you spend the most time with are at in life and see where you fall within that mix.

Maybe 3 of your 5 earn about $10,000 annually, the 4th earns about $18,00, the 5th about $30,000. 10,000 +

10,000 + 10,000 + 18,000 + 30,000 = 78,000/5 = $15,600 is the median off all of them, and there's a good chance you are earning around that median amount! Try is with your 5, it will be eerily accurate!

This doesn't just apply to money, but habits, lifestyle traits, and decision making. Those are the factors that influence our results. The people we spend the most time with, we tend to be the most like. We pick up the habits because we want to be like each other. Yes, we have our own wants, needs, and individuality, but how do we measure progress? By looking at those around us.

INFLUENCE

It's like this, imagine you're hanging out with one of your really successful friends, or you just met someone at work whose knocking it out of the park. Just being around them makes you feel like you can take on the world! They bounce back and forth creative ideas with you, share all their cool projects their working on; they're all around uplifting. You walk away so inspired, thinking, "Man, if he can do it, so can I! I'm going to go put together that rock band I always wanted to do!"

And then...

You hang out with one of your college buddies who never quite *'made it'* like they wanted to. They still talk about doing stuff, but they never actually *do* anything, it's always 'later' or 'tomorrow'. They complain about the things they don't like in their life, and you end up chiming in bitching about the stuff you don't like about yours. You leave their place thinking, "Ugh, I gotta do the dishes when I get home, life's so hard."

Our minds are great at justification, and given a readily available excuse, it'll tend to latch onto it. Likewise, when we have dreams and goals and ambitions, and someone is going for it, we'll latch onto the thought that it's possible for us too. Who you're spending the most time with, you'll be the most like.

DON'T TRY TO CHANGE 'EM

So, you might be thinking, "Crap, I've got friends that make me feel like I've conquered the world when I just clean my house..." that's ok. You are friends for a reason, there's something you enjoy about each other's company. As you start to work on living your best life, you're going through a lot of change – but do not try to change the people around you! You're ready for the change you're embarking on, they may not be.

The surest way to get people to do what you're doing anyway, is to lead by example. As you're living your best life and finding you're a happier healthier version of you, they may ask what you're doing anyhow. Then again, they may not.

TO SHARE OR NOT TO SHARE

While you're working on this new kick-ass version of yourself, the one thing we often want to do is tell all of our closest friends about this amazing new growth journey we're on. *Whoa there! Hold up!* Who you choose to tell is important.

If your main crowd aren't pushing towards living their dream life, you're probably going to be disappointed by the reactions you'll get. It's not that they're going to be mean about it (albeit you might have a friend that likes to be a sarcastic patronizing ding-dong) but generally speaking, we tend to get their fears smeared all over us: "What?! You're going to quit your secure job to be a rock band drummer?!

With a mortgage and two kids?!" or "You know most new businesses fail right?" or "Investing in real estate/stock market is a gamble, you know your returns aren't guaranteed right?"

Meanwhile OF COURSE YOU KNOW all of those things! You're already combating your own fear and insecurities that your subconscious is bubbling up and throwing at you. The very last thing you need is to have a bunch of other people remind you of it. Of course, they're saying it because they're worried, and also because it activates their own fear response. When you decide to get serious about going after your dream, you're holding up a big old mirror to everyone around you that reminds them that they aren't going after their dreams, so they try to pull you back down. It's easier to stop you from succeeding than it is for them to face their own crap and go hell-bent for glory after their dreams.

Now, on the other hand, if you've already surrounded yourself with a bunch of amazing people who are bringing it on their own growth journey, kicking butt, and taking names, yeah, share away! Those types of people want to see you grow and succeed! They will cheer you on, be inspired by you, and help assure you you're on the right track.

UPGRADING YOUR CIRCLE OF 5

Nope, you don't have to write up a bunch of break up letters. Your circle of 5 are the 5 people you spend the *most* time with. They aren't the only people in your life, they're the most influential people in your life. The important thing with this activity is making sure the people you're around the most are positive and achievers, so you're uplifted when you're around them.

A good rule of thumb: if you're the smartest person in the room, you're in the wrong room. We learn and grow from people who have done things we haven't, who are doing what we want to be doing. Seek out successful people in your desired field of interest. Remember, we're all human, don't count people "out of your league" and avoid reaching out. You never know what may happen, or who they may guide you to.

If you work in a position in a company and you're seeking to get into another area of work within the company, start spending time with the people who work in that area who are successful at it. See what they do, how they do it, what's their outlook? Surround yourself with the people you want to learn from.

If you've been spending the majority of your time with some negative nellies, just redirect your time to being with people who lift you up. If people drag your energy down when you're around them, spend less time with them. You don't have to ditch them, break up with them, or even explain yourself; you're busy working on new things – that's it! You can still see those people if you want to, you're just not spending the majority of your time with them anymore.

GROWING TOGETHER OR GROWING APART

We're always growing and changing, and as you embark on your personal transformation, you'll be undergoing a lot of big changes. You'll be growing in the mindset department, and when you grow there, your physical reality changes radically too. While this growth journey has no end, you'll notice along the way your life is changing, and with it your perspective and interests. You'll be more drawn to spending time with positive uplifting people, because they'll make you feel good and challenge you in new ways.

As you're growing and changing, the people around you are also changing in their own way. Your growth may inspire some to take great leaps and bounds of their own. For others, they may get caught in some downward spiral, or gain interests that you have no interest in. You may find at some point the people you were once really close to feel like strangers. Don't fear this, this is inevitable regardless of whether or not you we're pushing to become your best self. You just may notice it more acutely with your major changes.

I'm not saying people will up and leave you, I'm just saying you could find you've grown apart from someone along this path. The Universe brings people and things into our lives at the right place and time for us to learn and grown and experience what we need at that time. Life is transitory, so as you change, it may just happen that your relationships change too. It's OK. People might stay or go, just be you, shine your light, and see what happens. People in alignment with who you are becoming will be there, cheering you on every step of the way!

To-Do List

- Do the Sum of 5 Practice
- Make some new connections with people who are succeeding in the areas you want to succeed at
- Be at peace, knowing the people who are meant to be there will be

Chapter 10: Success Partner

If you've never had a success partner before, you are in for a treat! It can take a while to find the right person to be your success partner, and that's OK – don't rush it! So, what should you be looking for?

WHAT'S A SUCCESS PARTNER?

A Success partner is pretty much what it sounds like. It's kind of like an accountability buddy. They're a person who is working on their goals, usually similar goals to what you're working toward, who will push you and support you on your path to success, while you do the same for them. Your circle of 5 offers regular positivity, encouragement, and inspiration, while your success partner is more specifically helping you on a more regular basis.

WHAT YOU WANT IN A SUCCSS PARTNER

A success partner is a really personal thing. You want someone who you get along with, who's on the same page, who just *gets* you! You also want that person to be good at keeping you on track, encouraging you, and who isn't afraid to call you out when you need it. It's kind of like you want to find a bestie with a backbone, who is also a trail blazer.

Now, this is a relationship, so keep in mind the great connection part might take a while. Relationships take time to blossom, so if you meet someone and there aren't immediate fireworks going off, don't panic. In an initial conversation you want to see that they get your vision, that they have their own ambition, that you understand each other, and you feel like you can communicate well.

If you're talking to someone who is a complainer, or uncertain, or really caught up in doubt, move on. You'll constantly be lifting them up, and they'll constantly be dragging you down. Fear and doubt are part of the process but focusing on it spells disaster. No, you're not looking for perfection in a success partner, but you don't want a negative nelly either.

It can help sometimes to work someone with opposing skills. For example, if you're really bad at planning and structure, but incredibly creative, while your success partner is super organized but can never seem to brain storm anything, you can help each other out tremendously. Your strength is their weakness, and vice versa, so you can collaborate well, and overcome the areas that otherwise would hold you both back from progressing.

WHERE TO FIND A SUCCESS PARTNER

There are many different ways you may find a success partner to work with. There are lots of groups on social media sites where people are actively looking for success partners in. Put feelers out, and ask friends, family, and co-workers if they can recommend people they think might be a good fit. Put yourself in places successful like-minded people might be; library, country club, tea house or coffee shop, etc.

SETTING UP A ROUTINE WITH YOUR SUCCESS PARTNER

Knowing what you expect of each other is really important. Setting clear guidelines up front will help you both out in the long run. While your specific needs will vary based on what you're working on, here are some suggestions:

- Check-ins
  - Figure out how often you're going to touch base, daily, every other day, weekly, etc. and then stick to it.

- Challenge Each Other
    - We don't always push ourselves enough, so having our success partner throw a challenge our way can help us push harder than we otherwise would.
- Accountability
    - If you say you're going to do something, your success partner will hold you to it, and vice-versa. If there are no consequences, it's way easier to push things to the back burner. Figure out as each situation arises what happens if you don't hit your targets; you can create penalties like additional have to-dos. For example, if one of you commits to prospecting 100 new customers this week and only prospects 73, then the following week that person has to prospect 150. Above all, if you're not hitting crucial targets then your dream is further and further away, but have immediate consequences helps us feel the urgency!

- Positivity
  - On our journey to live our best life we are facing our own fears and dodging obstacles. Our mindset is the most important thing to see us through this storm of craziness. When you talk with your success partner, encourage and support them. Reassure them they're on the right track.
- Brainstorming
  - Two minds are better than one. Set time at least once a month to brainstorm new ideas together to help each other take their 'thing' to the next level of awesomeness!
- Celebrate the Wins
  - We work our tails of with these life-transformations! It's important to celebrate the wins along the way, as well as the big wins. Progress is progress, whether it's your first customer, or your first million dollars – celebrate every step together!

Add anything you need to onto this list that you feel would be helpful. Together you will be able to face challenges and overcome!

- **To-Do List**
    - Actively seek a success partner
    - When you find your success partner create a routine with them that is beneficial to you both

Chapter 11:

Personal Development

When you're making massive changes to your life, you need an ironclad mindset. Your inner most fears will be coming up, the people around you will share their doubt and concern, and on top of that the Universe likes to test just how serious you are about leaving your rickety life behind in search of greener pastures. Now before you slam this book shut and say, "You know what, that sounds awful, I think I'm actually OK with my mediocre life," it's not that bad. I mean, in the moment it may feel terrifying, but you're going to push through and come out on the other side and wonder why in the world it took you so long to make these changes!

It is also all about perspective! If you're bigger than your problems, then the problems don't even feel like problems. Think of it this way: you live on a planet that is flying through space at crazy high speeds, just the right distance from our star to support life. Our solar system is part of this huge galaxy, and this galaxy is part of a Universe that's bigger than out minds can even try to comprehend. Nothing – and I mean nothing – that can happen could possibly be that big of a deal in the grand scheme of the Universe. So, the next time you have some spilt milk, instead of crying about it, realize what a non-problem it is, deal with it, and move on!

To be the person you need to be to take on this new life, with all its badass goodness, and its challenges, you just need to grow. When you purposefully put effort into growing your mindset, everything around you changes. The daily habits you need to do to succeed feel easier, your attitude is better, that better attitude makes you more grateful, which means the Law of Attraction is at play in a big positive way for you all the time; it's this huge domino effect!

WAYS TO INCORPORATE PERSONAL DEVELOPEMENT

Reading

One of the easiest ways to start changing right now is through reading. It's easily accessible, books, great internet articles, blogs, etc. There's so much out there on every topic; business, finance, relationships, how to be a better friend/parent, spiritual growth, Law of Attraction, and so on and so forth. You can find out what it takes to achieve what you want through reading. My most important tip is don't just read it, apply it. Just reading it will still help you but applying it will radically change your life!

Audio

Turn your car into a university on wheels! Audio books, podcasts, taped interviews, etc. make it so easy to surround ourselves with knowledge when we're not able to read and just doing something mundane. Don't drive? Listen while you're going through your morning routine, in the shower, getting dressed, making coffee or tea, eating breakfast, etc. It doesn't take any extra time out of your day and can make a massive impact on your life!

Courses

Immersing in a course, be it online or in person, can help get your consistency down, and to push you to do the things you'd normally avoid or push off to a later date that never seems to roll around. When you're working within a group setting you don't want to let the people around you down; it encourages us to contribute to the whole. You also benefit from the insight and various perspectives of the other people you're doing the course with. On top of that having a teacher there to answer questions and clarify concepts helps you progress that much faster.

Just like books, there are courses and seminars on all sorts of topics, finance, romance, spiritual, family, relationships, career, etc. and of course they can get into really specific ones too like how to build a 1 million following for your dog's social media account, or whatever it is you want to do! Find an online course, or sign up for a seminar, that's going to push you to grow,

Coach

Imagine you're lost wandering through the woods, looking for your way out. You know what you want: to get out of the damn woods! But you don't know how to achieve it. You have no sense of direction, no idea how close you are to anything further than 20-30 feet in any direction. Your perspective is limited to seeing exactly what's before you and guessing on what's the best next step. You could make an educated guess and decide to walk directly in one direction until you get out, but maybe the direction you take will take 10 times longer than another.

A coach is like someone standing up on a cliff overlooking the forest you're fumbling through. They can see the lake 20 miles east of you, and the highway 5 miles north-west, and they can guide you to it. A coach is someone who has succeeded in the area you're trying to work at succeeding in. They can see the big picture, and help you make the right choices to get there, and get there faster, plus help you to avoid running into a bear attack along the way.

There are different kinds of coaches out there. Life coaches tend to focus on the big picture of all areas of your life, and then there are also coaches that focus specifically on one thing, like your love life, for example. Whatever you're looking for you can find the right person to help you. Whoever you choose, make sure they're successful at what you're trying to accomplish; getting financial advice from someone whose got tumbleweeds in their bank account isn't going to be beneficial.

Journaling

Getting your thoughts out on paper can be incredibly beneficial. It helps you to gain clarity, revisit thoughts, and get really clear about where you're headed. You can also work through any emotionally difficult situations, by writing out what has happened you, in essence, you can then release it. It also gives you a simple platform to brainstorm.

Get Moving

Physical exercise is a crucial component to personal growth. Your body is your one and only vehicle in this life, so it's important to take care of it in a well-rounded way. When you exercise, you have more energy, you can concentrate better, you get sick less frequently, you feel happier (yay endorphins!), and you have more confidence. It also works out the stress, and when you're massively transforming your life, there will be stresses to work out. Whether you sign up for a yoga class, go for a run, or plug into P90X, pick something, and make it a daily part of your routine.

Need some support? Come join our online fitness community: www.AmandaRoseFitness.com

Fuel

Just like exercise, what you eat effects your body. Your body is like a car, better fuel gives you more gas millage, and means less repairs. No, you don't have to go out and become a full-fledged nutritionist, but spend some time learning about food and how it effects the body. With the internet at our fingertips, the knowledge is just a few clicks away. Or, you can schedule in an appointment with a nutritionist to help figure out your own personal needs, or use nutritionist created 2B Mindset like our fitness support group does: www.AmandaRoseFitness.com

Sleep

If you're used to running off a little sleep and a lot of caffeine, it's time to get more Zzz time in. Your body needs sleep and caffeine isn't a substitute for it. Lack of sleep leads to lack of focus, leads to poor work performance, bad decisions, and quite often quitting. Your body can only take so much before it shuts down to replenish.

You need 8 hours a night; you've heard that before. The adult body needs 8 hours a night to have the proper amount of rest to reduce stress, give you better memory retention, help with your metabolism which helps prevent obesity, prevent depression, and when you're well rested and less grouchy you're better at socializing. There's a whole slew of other benefits, from numerous studies done over the years.

Sure, there's the odd time on this path to creating something incredible, with life-changing impact, where you might need to pull an all-nighter, go to bed super late or get up super early, but I'm talking about more often than not sleeping enough. Study after study shows us the benefits of getting in enough sleep, and the detriments of not. Now before you start throwing out the excuses on why you can't, *my kids wake me up early, I've got too much to do, my cat shoves her butt hole in my face if I'm not up to feed her, etc.* we all have reasons not to do the things we need to do. You can make it happen, it just may take some reworking.

First, I want to tackle that all holy "I'm too busy," excuse because it's getting old. North Americans in particular wear "I'm too busy," like it's some sort of badge of honor, like their self-worth is tied into having a ton of stuff to do. Statistics still show American's watch an average of 3-5 hours of television a night, so clearly not everyone is that swamped. How much is actually necessary and how much is just busy work? We see in a lot of other countries around the world shorter work days and higher productivity. A happier well rested person can get more done in a more efficient way and enjoy their life. You can have both.

A lot of other reasons are just requiring some scheduling creativity. Your cat wakes you up for breakfast at the crack of dawn? Get a programable pet food dispenser that will feed them, so you don't have to get up. Kids wake you up? Go to bed earlier or talk to your spouse about taking care of them so you can get in some extra shut-eye (maybe offer to trade off). Need to get up early while you're still working your day job? Again, go to bed earlier. Find a way to make it happen.

If you're used to getting in 4-5 hours of sleep a night, work your way up. Add an hour a week until you're up to 8. If insomnia is an issue, see your doctor, go to a clinic, get some white noise maker, meditate before bed; work on it until you find what helps. Some people need extra melatonin, others just have busy brain and need something to focus on to shut their brain down.

The bottom line? Get that shut eye in. Living your best life depends on it.

Balance

All or nothing just doesn't work. Being all about work, or all about family, or all about a new hobby, or all about time with friends, it leaves this feeling of being incomplete. It can make you feel like you have things on your plate yet to be done when you're only focused on one thing. You'll be happier, and feel more accomplished, when you balance things out.

Now quite often people think of balancing as being all about time allotment, and that's not the case. One day you might need to put in 10 hours on work, and only have 2 hours with your family, and 10 minutes to yourself. The balance comes from the quality of time you're spending on each thing. If you're on your phone the entire time with your family, you won't feel like you've really spent time with them at all. Be present in the moment with whatever or whoever you're with, and you will feel a greater satisfaction and happiness.

Make time for what's important. If you never make time for certain people or activities, it won't just magically appear. If you leave something important to, "If I've got time later," you won't do it. You have to make the time for the things that are important to you.

- **To-Do List**
    - Choose 3 things from the list above to start doing tomorrow
    - Set timelines for implementing the rest

Chapter 12: Coach

We briefly talked about the benefits of having a coach in the last chapter, and now we're going to dive into that some more.

As human beings we tend to be naturally... lazy. We also all have our own comfort zone level. Even those that consider themselves driven will find themselves avoiding and procrastinating certain things they dislike doing. If you're self-governing, this can prove detrimental to progress.

When we set goals for ourselves, and then break down what needs to be done we often are battling our subjective view. If you set a goal of prospecting 100 new potential clients this week, but making the phone calls stresses you out, you'll most likely find a bunch of 'busy work' to pre-occupy yourself with. That busy work makes it *feel* like you're working, when you're really avoiding what needs to be done to reach your goal. Then midway through the week when you've only pushed yourself to make 1 call, you push the deadline back another week.

A coach is going to help you identify your strengths and your weaknesses. They will be able to take your goal to the next level, by objectively looking at it and determining what needs to be done. Your coach can help you set more challenging deadlines and give you the support and motivation to hit them. Your coach can also effectively see what needs to be delegated, and what you personally need to handle to create the most impact. This kind of accountability and insight will help you to grow exponentially faster.

THE BEST DON'T DO IT ALONE

Olympic athletes, CEOs, Singers, Actors, etc. don't make it to the top without help. An athlete doesn't just get to arbitrarily practice when the mood beseeches them and then take home the gold medal, they have to get plugged into a regime, stick to it on the days when they reaaaally don't feel like it, and work harder in their weak areas. To hone and perfect your skills, you need a good coach who can work with you to get you to improve.

DISCIPLINE

I'm a big fan of self-discipline, but we all have our own idea of what's "good enough." When you bring in a coach to help you get better, they raise the bar. You get a whole new level of discipline; now you're not only not letting yourself down, you're not letting your coach down. You also are getting the benefit of someone who knows exactly what it's going to take for you to hit that next level, to win the gold, take home the Grammy, get CEO award of the year, win the bake sale, retire from your crap job, and live the life you've always wanted.

It's hard adapting to a new routine, especially if you're head strong, but change always feels this way at first. Before you know it, it'll feel like you've always trained this way. You'll see marked improvements in your performance and realize just how much more you're capable of!

COMFORT ZONE

Most people never venture outside of their comfort zones, cause, it's really cozy in there. You're never overly challenged, and never have to worry about failure while you're in that little area. But it is little, and confining, and nothing remarkable ever happens their either. What a boring place to live.

Some people with big goals will push themselves to break the confines of their comfort zone. It's painful, there's a lot of pep talk, and it's the equivalent of slowly getting into a pool when the water is really cold, and you're wondering, "Should I really swim today? Maybe it'll be warmer tomorrow..." and you keep testing the first step, ankle deep.

People with ambitions plus a phenomenal coach push the boundaries. They have their coach to say to them, "Hey, everything you ever wanted is in that pool! It's going to be shocking at first, then feel amazing! You need to get into that pool, now! GO!" and you don't get to walk in, your coach has you jump in. It is shocking, but then your body adapts, and you're floating, and it feels amazing!

PLANNING

Sometimes we get in our own way with indecisiveness. What's the next best step? Should I do this, this, or this? Doubt creeps in, procrastination steps in, and nothing gets accomplished. A coach can look at your big picture and help you action-plan accordingly. Your coach will know what needs to happen first, so you don't put the cart before the proverbial horse.

MOTIVATION

We're all motivated by a reason, our *why*, which is the driving force when the going gets tough. When you work with a coach you're going to share this with them, and they're going to remind you of it on those hard days when all you can see is what looks like a million hurdles ahead. Your coach is going to keep you focused on what's really important, so you don't quit.

Your coach is also going to see things in you, your strengths, and the victories along the way, and they will remind you of how far you've come. They want to see you succeed and will be cheering you on as you grow on your journey. A coach helps you realize you're stronger than you ever thought you were!

EXPONENTIAL RETURNS

A coach is an investment, there's no doubt, but a great coach will be worth their weight in gold. A coach's help can help you fast track your success and create massive returns. It's also another way for you to tell the Universe, "I am freakin' serious about this dream of mine!" because it's another form of taking action towards your goal.

- **To-Do List**
    - Start looking for a coach who is the right fit to help you
    - Interview your top picks; call them and see who you resonate with
    - Decide on a coach and hire them

Chapter 13: Present

We are so good at re-hashing the past, and fretting about the future, that we have a damn hard time being present in the moment. When our mind is living in the past, or trying to predict the future, we're missing out on what's happening right now. Right now is all there really is. You can't change the past, and the future hasn't happened yet.

Living in the past makes you feel Depressed

Living in the future makes you feel Anxious

Living in the moment makes you feel at Peace

When you learn to be present, you are more in tune with everything happening around you. The Universe can't just pick up the phone and call us for a chat and to directly give us information, instead it communicates to us through subtler methods. If your mind is anywhere but present in this moment, you're very likely to miss the message.

When you're present in the moment, and picking up the Universal cues, your life radically changes. You're in the flow, and everything begins to fall into place. It's an incredible experience when you're in tune with the Universe.

Use these methods to work on being more present in the moment:

JUST BE

This is so much easier said than done. We are always going 100 miles an hour getting things done. Taking a moment to just be, to do nothing, and take in the moment, is not something we're accustomed to. Set a timer on your phone to go off every 2 hours and take that moment to just be in your surroundings. Notice the sights, sounds, and smells, and remind yourself that this moment is the only one that matters.

MEDITATE

Meditation is one of the easiest ways to get yourself to be present in the moment. Meditation is all about releasing your thoughts and focusing in on your breath, which allows you to listen to cues from your Higher Self and the Universe. Mediation is of course a practice, meaning it's simple but it's not easy.

You can meditate for 3 minutes or 3 hours, there's no right or wrong length of time. Set a timer for whatever length of time you've chosen; this will keep you from thinking about how much time has elapsed and allow you to relax into the meditation. You can meditate sitting down or lying down, although if you're prone to easily drift into sleep while lying down then opt in for sitting.

Get your body in a comfortable position. If sitting, often cross legged in most comfortable, and helps to support the spine. Hands can rest of the thighs of knees. Close your eyes and begin to focus on your breathing.

You can breathe normally simply through the nose, or breath in through the nose and exhale through the mouth. Your thoughts will creep into our mind while you meditate, it's normal, and nothing to get upset about. Acknowledge the thoughts when they arise and then gently let them go. Some days will be easier than others. Continue to focus on the breath until your timer goes off and notice any thoughts that come up for later contemplation.

Optionally before meditating you can ask the Universe a question. You may or may not find the answer comes during the meditation, but you've opened up communications, and will likely find the answer comes to you either during or after the meditation.

BREATHE

Our breath is our lifeline. Of all the things our body needs to live, we'd die soonest from lack of oxygen. Our breath is vital to our existence, and it can be used to center ourselves when we're feeling overwhelmed or unfocused. At any moment, no matter what we're doing, we can take stock using our breath.

One of the simplest things we can do to find our center using our breath is to do a slow count inhale, a slow count hold, and a slow count exhale. It gives the mind something to focus on, you can feel the air replenishes your body, and the way it invigorates your mind. This simple act will immediately help you to become present in the moment, melt away stress, and give you better concentration on the task at hand.

ANIMAL GUIDANCE

There are no better masters of the art of living in the moment than animals. Our animal friends live completely in the present, which allows them to fully enjoy and experience what's happening. They're not stuck dwelling on the past, or worried about the future, they're living right here in the *now*.

This ability allows them to fully experience the joy of doing whatever they're doing. You ever notice how cats can completely relax into sleep? Unlike humans, their brains aren't worriedly running rampant when they want some shut eye. Or how a dog gets just so over-the-moon excited when you walk in the door? It's like you, and the dog, and that moment, are the best thing that ever was and ever will be.

If you've got a pet spend more time being with them. Learn from their wisdom of being present. You'll feel better and have a lot more fun spending more time in their presence. If you don't, try to get outside, watch a bird, or a squirrel do their thing and marvel in the fun of it all!

UNLOAD YOUR MIND

Keeping your to-do list, your fears, your goals, and how pissed off you are about that parking ticket earlier, all up in your thoughts is incredibly inefficient, not to mention stressful! If you're constantly having to wonder what you have to do next, and are wandering aimlessly, it's time to get organized. Getting things out of your mind and on to paper will make it feel like the world was just lifted off of your shoulders. Add to that talking to a good friend, your spouse, a therapist, or your success partner, about your feelings so you can release them, and *bam!* You are unstoppable!

First things first, if you didn't go through the goal writing exercise earlier in this book and said, "I can do that all in my head," go back now and do it written-down right now. Your mind is less efficient when it has to keep remembering the same thing over and over, which means you have less cognitive function during the doing. Then, when you have your goals written-down you can extrapolate your to-do list by reverse engineering what needs to be done to get there. Write out your daily to-do list or use a to-do list app and use it! Give your brain a break from having to carry the entire load.

Next, keeping your feelings all bottled up will make you feel like you're living in the past, and in constant terror of all the things that can happen in the future. Having a daily journal to just unload can help, and it's often incredibly helpful to talk to somebody. We get to have a cathartic experience, have someone tell us that yes, we are being ridiculous, and that our fears are unfounded.

Once you take all of these space-taking thoughts out of your head, you'll be able to be aware in the moment. You won't feel overwhelmed and out of control, because you know what you need to do from your list, and you'll feel centered because you're not re-hashing emotional situations because you will have able to let them go by journaling and talking it out. These are simple things to do that make a huge impact on our mental state.

- **To-Do List**
    - Choose 2 things from the list above to implement today to help yourself be more present in the moment
    - Set time lines for implementing the rest

Chapter 14: Sales

Uh, sales? I thought this was about living my best life? It is, and that's why we have this very important topic to cover. If you want to live your best life, your dream life, you have to get good at sales. I don't care what you're pursuing, this invaluable skill is necessary.

BREAKING THE STIGMA

What People Imagine Sales is Like

The words, *sales, salesman, saleswoman,* have been dirtied up. They have been made out to be filthy, and gross, and something to avoid at all cost. This negative perception is costing millions... no *billions* of people not to go after their dream life.

When we hear the word *salesman*, it instantly conjures up this image of this sleaze-ball, used car salesmen, who is going to sell you a lemon. Pretty much, right? Of course, there's the odd dirt bag out there selling snake oil, but more often than not sales are incredible positive experiences. That's what they *should* be! And when the positive ones happen, you don't even associate the word 'sales' to it!

What Sales Really is Like

The core of what sales are really about is about helping someone else. That's it's essence. It is helping them to see why your idea, your solution, will be beneficial to them. Everyone sells every single day, whether they realize it or not.

Parents have to sell their kids on the idea of eating their vegetables, cleaning their rooms, manners, etc. When you're choosing what movie to watch with your spouse or a friend, you're persuading them on why your choice would be enjoyable. When you show up at work, you're selling your skills to your boss and your clients and co-workers. Actors have to sell casting directors on their performance abilities in an audition. It doesn't matter who you are, or what you're doing, you're selling something to somebody; whether it's an idea, a product, or a service, you're selling.

To sell is a subtle thing, and it happens in most conversations. When you help people get what they want, you get what you want too. Everybody wins!

THE MOST IMPORTANT PIECE

What's the most important part of business? Not marketing, not great customer service, not manufacturing; it's sales. Why? Without sales, there is no money. No money means you can't pay for marketing, or those customer service reps, or manufacturing, or to keep the freaking lights on! Sales are the key to success in any business endeavor.

SKILL

Selling is a skill, like any other. It's something you can learn, and you already have a baseline from day-to-day life to work from. So, let's cover some important aspects...

It's All About Them

If you try to make a sale, you won't. Your intention when you set out is paramount. Trying to sell something makes it all about you and what you're offering. Nobody cares about you or what you're selling, they care about... you guessed it, their own needs.

If you want to be incredible at sales (AKA use a necessary skill to build your dream life) then you need to put other people's needs first when you talk to them. Find out who they are, and what problem do they have that you can help them with. They have a problem, and your idea, product, or service, may be the solution.

Asking questions is the number one way to find out about them and their needs. Get good at asking questions. The questions you ask will of course vary pending on where you are, and who you're talking to, however it never hurts to ask how someone's doing. Break the ice by showing them you're a human being, and that you're there to help.

Let Go of the Guilt

When someone is new to sales, they tend to have this awkwardness or guilt about being paid for a sale. It's like they feel really bad about it because...? Who knows. Really there's no reason to feel bad, if you're selling a legit idea, product, or service, you should know that when you help someone with it that you're improving their life in some way – and sometimes profoundly!

We're masters of creating fictional scenarios in our heads about just about everything. Maybe you've built it up in your head that you feel like when you make a sale you're basically robbing money from them. While, yes, they're paying for what you're offering, it's not like you pick-pocketed them for crying out loud! You offered what you had, explained how it'd benefit them based on their needs, and they made the decision that you were right!

Think about a time when you recommended a product or service to someone you care about that you didn't profit from. Something you tried and loved and knew that they're love to! It made you feel all good and giddy when they agreed to buy it, because you knew how much joy it'd bring to them. Selling is the exact same and should feel the exact same, you just happen to get paid too!

Your income from sales is directly proportionate to the number of people you're helping. If you're making more money, then you're helping more people positively change their lives. It's that simple.

Don't Be Shy

Insecurity and self-doubt just waste everybody's time. If you have an idea, product, or service, that will benefit others, don't be selfish and keep it to yourself! Share! You're going to be told no and you're going to be told yes. You have to get through the rejection to get to the person who goes, "Oh my gosh, take my money, I freakin' need that in my life! Thank you!"

We're so often our own worst critics. Don't try and pre-judge how what you're offering will affect others, or what their reaction will be to it. Let's say for example you're selling an ultra-light non-stick cooking pan. You could get right into doubt about it, "Who the heck needs another frying pan? Everybody already has one! And non-stick isn't new..." Little do you know the person you offer it to has terrible arthritis that's prevented them from cooking, which has been a life-long passion of their, and this new ultra-light pan is going to allow them to get back in the kitchen. Or maybe that other person has a kid going off to college and they just gave their kid a ton of kitchen things and now they need new pans. The thing is, you just don't know – so tell everybody!

PRACTICE

Nobody is an expert right out of the gate on anything. It takes time to learn and hone this skill, just like any other. Practice makes perfect, and you'll learn more from failure than you will from success. The thing to remember is that failing is a good thing. Failing means you're trying something new, and as long as you can objectively look at what happened and learn from it, failure is how you'll grow and get better.

CONTINUE TO LEARN

Just like practicing, you'll want to continue to learn new skills. If you're in an actual sales position within a company, go on sales calls with other successful sales people. If you're doing your own thang, then get some books and audio tapes on the subject. There's so much excellent advice out there from some truly inspirational people, go soak it up!

- **To-Do List**
    - Let go of any negative preconceptions you have about sales
    - Set out to learn about and get great at sales

Chapter 15: Social Media

We have this incredibly amazing tool available to us, to connect us to the world. Social media is a major component, not just of modern life, but modern marketing. In our endeavors in life, we can't do it alone, we need other people to help us. Social media makes for a wonderful way to reach those other people who are in alignment with you.

I'll be honest, I wasn't a fan of social media at first. I got arm twisted in college to sign up for a few accounts on major platforms, but I rarely went on them for years. It only ever looked like a drama hub, or somewhere people pretentiously posted how amazing their lives were – *No thank you!*

Then in 2013 I set out to start a home fitness business in network marketing, and lo and behold, I needed social media. I got over myself and my *above-it-all* attitude towards social media and set out to learn. If this was the way to make my dreams a reality, I was going to embrace it and use it.

Little did I know social media marketing would be much more complicated than I expected. Target markets, algorithms, my brand, calls to action... *what the hell is a hashtag?* There was a lot to learn.

I just fumbled and failed a lot at first. I put up gross salesy posts with purchase links. No surprise, no likes, comments, shares, or... sales. It wasn't working, and that in and of itself, was incredibly helpful. So, I stopped doing those posts and tried something new. I failed repeatedly and then, I started to get some traction.

My learning was very trial-and-error based at first, but as I grew as a person and an entrepreneur, I started to actually study social media. I got books, watched webinars, learned from successful people in our company; I made it my job to learn about it. This second approach will save you lots of stress and guessing at why your posts aren't making an impact as you get going.

Here is a foundation of helpful Dos and Don'ts to get you started!

HOW TO SHARE ON SOCIAL MEDIA TO GET INTERACTION

Finding your voice on social media is an important part of social media marketing. Your ideal clients, EI. your target market, will respond to your posts when your message matters to them. There are some also some steadfast do's and don'ts as well, so we're going to start there.

DON'Ts

Old School Blunt Marketing Tactics Don't Work

Even for big brand name companies, the appeal of the classic ad is... dead. People don't want to be force fed tacky overused slogans *'buy this'* or *'your life will be so much better when you do this'* kind of advertising. We were inundated by it as a culture, and now we're over it.

Don't Pretend to be Someone You're Not

Getting ideas from other successful people in your field is one thing but copying them is going to hurt you in the long run. We often look up to the people at the top, even want to be them at times, but when we try to pretend to be them, while in the short term you may see gains, ultimately, as you grow as a leader, you'll feel inauthentic.

Then your audience will feel that. And then if you change your message and shine on as your true badass self (like you should be doing from the get-go), the people who liked you for who you aren't will trickle off, and you'll have to start from scratch. Embrace who you are and be loud and proud about it!

Me, me, me, me, me!

There's nothing more... *awful*, than someone constant showboating. If all I ever see is how freaking fantastic you are, that you fart rainbows, and piss apple juice, then I'm out.

Done. Bye. Unfollow.

Now don't get me wrong, it can be about you. Your audience does want to get to know who you are and what you're all about but be humble and be a giver. What can you contribute in your posts to help others out? Lift them up and give them a reason to want to cheer you on!

Manifesting Your Best Life

DOs

Be Vulnerable

Perfection doesn't exist, and people seeing someone as 'perfect' will make someone scrolling by think, "Wow, good for her! But I could never do that..." Or you know, they might just think, "Eesh, bitch," and keep scrolling.

What have you struggled with and overcome? What was hard for you that others might be struggling with? Sharing how you overcame struggles people are currently dealing with gives them the strength to overcome too. Don't be selfish, share that stuff!

Be Down to Earth

When people google about celebrities, the most common thing they want to know is what they wear to the grocery store. Not how many awards they have, their net worth, or any of that stuff... they want to see them doing their day to day lives. You might go, "Ugh, but I'm boring!" well think again. If people look up to you, and want to be you, they want to know that you're a regular human being too.

Give Advice your Followers Actually care About

What does your following care about? What are they struggling with? What advice/tips/tricks can you give them to help them out? Give them a reason to keep coming back to your page!

#Hashtag

If you're not hash tagging you're going to have a really hard time attracting new people. Hashtags create hyperlinks. When someone goes to a search bar and types "pets" it'll pull up all the posts that have the hashtag #pets on it. It makes you easy to find for your potential clients.

Your deal hashtags are going to be based on your target audience. Using their likes and interests, you can figure out what they would be searching for on social media. Hashtag those things so when they search, they find you!

Call to Action

You've got an incredible page, the right followers, people want to work with you... so let them know how! People need direction. if there's one thing that baffles my mind, it's when someone has this kickass social media page, but they never have a CTA (Call to Action) to let their followers know how to take the next step to work with them! At the end of your posts, let people know what to do next, whether it's commenting, visiting a web link, sending you a private message, etc. let them know what to do!

Be Consistent

A social media page is like a store front. People will start to expect your posts, and if you aren't consistent, your audience will take their business elsewhere. Think about it, if you showed up to a chain restaurant at 1PM on a Wednesday when they're always supposed to be open, you would be pretty peeved if they were unexpectedly closed.

So, don't post 5 times Monday, 0 times Tuesday, 0 times Wednesday, 1 time Thursday, 2 times Friday, 7 times Saturday, and 0 times on Sunday. It's better to post once daily than to be all over the map throughout the week. Whatever you choose, stick to it!

Who am I?

Finding your voice might sound like a really hard thing to do. But really, deep down, you know who you are, your morals and values, and the message you have to share with the world. The key about this is not second guessing yourself. This is really just a step of bravery, because when you're openly your authentic self on social media, you can feel like you've left yourself open for ridicule. We all know those internet trolls can be ruthless. But for everyone of those trolls 100 or a 1000 other people could benefit from you being brave enough to speak your truth. It's worth the one jerk you have to block every so often.

Be brave. Be you. Listen to your audience and be dedicated to bringing them the best experience ever!

- **To-Do List**
  - Be dedicated to learning how to use social media effectively

Chapter 16: The Zone

Zone, Vortex, Flow; whatever you call it, when you're in this state, it's pure magic. When we say we're "In the Zone," it's referring to a feeling, a feeling of being connected, of things falling into place with seemingly effortless ease. Our frequency is high, and the Universe is responding by bringing the people, places, and things we need into our line of sight with seemingly perfect timing.

While this can really feel magical, it's really that YOU have raised your vibe, set your intention, and strengthened your faith muscle so much that you're attracting everything with ease. Manifesting becomes easy and joyful when we are in the zone! The trick is getting there.

We've all experienced this state at some point, and often more than once, during our lives. When we've gotten all excited, laser focused, dedicated to make something happen, and most importantly, had unshakeable belief that it would come to fruition. Maybe it was getting that first job, a marriage proposal, making the basketball team in high-school, getting into the dream college or University, winning the art competition, getting the perfect haircut, acing the test, making the perfect brownie – whatever it was, when it happened, it felt incredible!

THE POWER OF DECISION

When we decide something is going to happen, watch out world, because *it is on!* To make a decision is to cut off all other options. There's no quitting, no ho-hum about changing our mind; we are committed! When that choice has been made, man oh man, do things ever start to fall into place!

There's something about deciding on something, that once we're all in, our mind can totally focus on making it happen. We become problem solving geniuses. The creativity is flowing, we take action, and we can move mountains!

One massive problem is... most people refuse to make a decision. They make excuses that they're trying to figure out the ins and outs, fumbling around with ideas for years, when really, they are just afraid to commit, struggling with the questions: "What if I fail?" "What if I succeed?" "What if it turns out bad?" "What will people think of me?"

When really, the question they should be asking is, "What if I never try?"

IF YOU DON'T TRY YOU HAVE ALREADY FAILED

Remember that: *If you don't try, you've already failed*. If you try, you have a chance to succeed. This is the reality of the situation right here. You'll never have every single detail of information before you begin, so stop trying to use it as an excuse. Have your idea, do a little research (set a time limit), then decide and fully commit. You'll adjust as you go. Success isn't a straight line, it's a bunch of ups and downs and learning and readjusting.

THE UNIVERSE HAS YOUR BACK

When you've taken a leap of faith, made a decision, and a freakin' going for it, the Universe is there for you to support you. The biggest hurdle is waiting, while believing it's going to happen – and really believing, not just hoping. See it as if it's already happened and act as if it's already yours, that's the key. When you've had the idea, made the decision, taken action, act as if you've got it, and have rock-solid faith that the Universe will be there at the right time to show you the How.

HOW TO GET IN THE FLOW

Being in the flow is an incredible state, one we tend to dip in and out of, and generally don't sit in too long. When we're in the flow we're connected to our higher-self, the Universe, Spirit, God, whatever you want to call it, and it's an energetic connection that we can almost feel. Some people can stay in this state longer than others. Life's many happenings tend to pull us out of that state as our awareness can only encapsulate so much at any given time. It will also, upon completion of making something happen, naturally dissipate.

Like anything, it's good to practice getting in the zone. Get to know what it feels like, and what it's like having that connection to the Universe. When you are able to tap in more easily, then when you're consciously shifting your life you can regularly tap in. Doubt and fear will feel less prominent because you know you're not alone, and manifesting will become much more seamless.

Try out some of these methods to practice getting into the flow:

MEDITATION

To Meditate: Sit in a quiet place. Focus on your breathing. Release your thoughts.

Meditation; the more you practice, the more you'll find yourself able to use this practice tap into the vortex while you're sitting there in silence. It takes time to get there, especially if you've got a busy mind. You might slip into it, and then realize you did, and then fall right out. It's OK, all part of the practice. Some days you might not tap in at all and can't stop thinking about how you have to go and get the laundry after you're done, and others you'll have a profound experience.

DIVINATION

To Divine: Tarot, Pendulum, Scry, Dowsing rods, Ruins

Divination allows us ask questions directly of the Universe and gives the Universe a way to respond back that we can understand or interpret. There are many different forms of divination, as you can see from the list above. Tarot cards have assigned meanings, each deck has a corresponding guidebook, and there are different card spreads you can use based on your question. Ruins are similar to Tarot, in that they have assigned meanings as well.

Using a pendulum or dowsing rods gives us "yes", "no", and "maybe" answers. When using either, test it by asking some questions you know the answer to, such as:

"Is my name _____?"

"Am I ___ years old?"

"Is my hair color _____?"

These baseline questions will allow you to determine the yes and no responses from each item. No movement at all will mean "maybe" or indecision.

Finally scrying, asking a question and looking into a bowl of water. This is best if the bowl is dark, so you can better see any imagery that may appear. When we scry, we hold the bowl in our hands, ask our question, and gaze into the water for our answer. This can take some time, and you may not see anything at first. This technique is best for someone with practice at divination and connecting to the Universe.

Intuition and trusting your feelings is a big part of any form of divination. Learn to trust that inner voice. When you're relaxed, and calm is the best time to divine. Remember, we're all energy, and we can sense how different energies feel, so work on taking time to get used to how things feel.

GET QUIET

To get quiet: Tell your thoughts to bugger off

Just taking a moment to shut off the mental chatter can help us to get grounded in the moment and be available to understand nudges from the Universe. When we're all go-go-go, stressed, and multi-tasking a million things, it's impossible for us to hear any gentle guidance from the Universe. When we're that busy, and if we stay that busy for a prolonged time, the nudges get more forceful until they become hard shoves, like getting sick or getting into a car accident. One way or another the Universe will be heard, so why not just slow down for a minute and listen?

A moment of getting quiet can not only alleviate the anxiety of everything you're trying to do, it gives you perspective and lets you get in the flow. When you're in that state new ideas can come, and suddenly you've discovered a way to delegate your massive to-do list, or how to start your own business so you're happier, or that you really do need that vacation cause you're burnt out. So many different things can happen when we're in that zone, it's a moment of clarity that's invaluable. So, take that moment to listen in.

CRYSTALS

To use crystals: Hold a crystal

Crystals are incredible. They are like compact energy nuggets! Crystals resonate at varying frequencies, there are tons of books and information on the web about the different energies around each crystal, so you can decide which ones are best for you at any given time. For example, if you're focused on love energies a rose quartz crystal would be a perfect fit.

When you pick up a crystal, you can feel it's subtle energies. Because of their conductive nature, it can help you to focus in on what you're trying to manifest. A crystal point is a great way to transmit and receive thought to and from the Universe. Think of a crystal like an amplifier.

SURRENDER

To Surrender: Trust and Release

Quit possibly the hardest yet simplest, and quite frankly, most powerful ways to get into the zone. When we know what you want, and we want it SO BADLY, we can end up pushing what we want away. Need comes from a place of lack, the idea of "I don't have it." If we're trying to be control freaks and to force something to happen, we end up spinning our wheels.

Surrendering is to let go of your way, to know what you want, and to be open to the "How" to be presented to you from the Universe. If you're building a life you've never lived, you don't know what that looks like. Be open to being shown the way. It's important as well to adapt the mantra, "This or something better!" We can only see a super tiny fraction of what's going on, but the Universe sees it all, so allow it the ability to bring you your vision – or – something even better that you never knew existed!

To surrender is to trust. This comes back to working on your faith in the Universe. Remind yourself of times before when you've seamlessly manifested things in your life and remember that the Universe is there for you! Let go of your death grip and allow yourself to be guided.

- **To-Do List**
  - Choose 1 technique for getting in the zone to do today
  - Choose at least 2 other techniques to try and set timelines to implement them

Chapter 17:

Believing is Seeing

Whoever said, "Seeing is believing," got is backwards. Thought is the prelude to anything showing up in the physical world. It is the reason you're always hearing the ever famous, "Thought Become Things," quote, being repeatedly spouted by anyone who has started to implement the Law of Attraction in their life. Once you've tried it, and seen it work, you're hooked!

Very simply put, the Law of Attraction states that what we focus on we attract into our lives. We are all energy. You, me, the sky, your home, your desk, plants, money, animals, and... the entire Universe. When you think any thought, neurons fire in your brain, this energy is reflected out to the Universe, and that energy is reciprocated. Therefore, if you're thinking about it, be ready for it to show up on your doorstep.

If you've always been a "I'll believe it when I see it," kind of person, then here's what I'm going to ask you...

1. In order to see it, you're going to need to believe it, so can you think of it as an experiment and let go of your doubt and go all in?

2. Can you think to a time in your life when you clearly visualized something, and it happened? It could be anything – getting a parking spot, the girl or guy you asked out saying yes, finding money you needed, getting the job, etc.

3. If you're not living the life of your dreams already, is it not worth giving it a shot? Besides a little bit of time, you ain't got nothing to lose.

4. Take a look at the many success stories out there using the Law of Attraction. There's something you can see to bolster your belief. Now it's your turn to change your life!

Here are some simple ways to get your mind focused on manifesting what you really want, instead of manifesting on auto-pilot:

GRATITUDE

Gratitude is the easiest thing to whip out at any given moment to manifest with. Here's why:

- You're always manifesting, with every thought, so as soon as you dip into gratitude you start manifesting the things that you actually want
- You can't be grateful and unhappy simultaneously, they're opposing emotions
- Gratitude gets you to think about and feel into what you want

There are 2 Ways to Use Gratitude...

Grateful for What I Have

Being grateful for what you have helps to put things in perspective, as well as to let the Universe know that, "Yes please, I'd like more of that!" There are so many things to be thankful for, it's staggering. For one, if you're reading this book you had some money to buy it, or someone gifted it to you, plus you have the time to read. Do you have a roof over your head? Fresh, clean water? Food? A job? Friends? Family? How about your senses that let you experience this world? Your organs that keep you alive? The fact that we live on a rock, spinning around a sun at an alarming velocity, just the right distance away to be not too hot and not too cold, with an atmosphere that supports life, in a solar system, in a galaxy, that's in a Universe that is SO BIG we cannot even comprehend it? We are alive and experiencing this crazy journey we call life; that is something to be thankful for.

Grateful for What Is to Come

Coming back to believing is seeing, you can use gratitude to be thankful *as if* you've already received what you want. This is incredibly powerful, and lets the Universe know that you are ready. Think about what you want and imagine it as if you got it. How would you feel? Get deep into that feeling. Your feelings amp up your energy, so the more you can get all in a tizzy about it the better!

VISUALIZATION

Visualization goes hand-in-hand with being grateful for what is to come. By picturing in your mind, with as much detail as you can muster, what it will be like to experience receiving what you're trying to manifest, in conjunction with being grateful for it, you're magnetizing that vision to you. Imagine really living through it. Here are some helpful questions to get you to picture, in the most detail possible, your dream coming to fruition:

- Where are you when you get the news?
- What is surrounding you in this space?
- How do you find out?
- Who is the first person you tell?
- How do you feel?
- What sensory things are you experiencing (taste, touch, smell, see, hear)?
- What's the first thing you do after getting the news?
- What do you do to celebrate?

AFFIRMATIONS

Affirmations are statements we remind ourselves of so that we stay focused on what we want to attract. They are often replacing old, negative beliefs, with new supportive ones. Like gratitude, it's something you can whip out anytime, anywhere, and refocus your mindset with.

2 Ways to Use Affirmations...

Use it to Set your Mindset and Focus at the Beginning of the Day with Affirmations

Your mindset when you start the day sets the entire pace for the rest of the day. So, when you wake up it's the ideal time to go over your affirmations – and you can do it while you're just going about your morning routine, brushing your hair and teeth, and getting dressed for the day. It will help you to not only feel better, but you're already focusing in on what you're wanting to attract to your life. Do this daily and you'll see big changes.

Use Affirmations to Change a Negative Dialogue

If you find your inner dialogue is flipping into old negative patterns, "I've always had bad luck," "I'm always broke," "All the good guys are taken," take stock, and reframe into what you want to start having happen instead, "I have good luck," "Money is all around me," "There are billions of amazing people on this planet and the right guy is out there for me!"

Affirmations

You can make up your own affirmations, and at the end of the day, it's most important that it feels good and right when you use them. Here are some of my favorite regulars, if you love 'em use 'em, and if not have fun creating your own. You can also get more specific based on your situation and individual desires.

"I am a money magnet!"

"Money comes to me easily and effortlessly!"

"I am loved!"

"I am worthy of love!"

"I am healthy!"

"I love my work!"

"I have lots of free time!"

"I am happy!"

MORNING GRATITUDE PRACTICE

I'm a big fan of having a morning gratitude practice. It can be big or small, but no matter the size it's powerful. When we begin the day by getting our mindset in the right place, and when we do it on a regular basis, our lives change drastically. If you want to see change, incorporate this!

You can structure your morning practice however you'd like and chose how long it will be. If you've read Manifesting on Purpose, pull it out and take a look at the day 6 practice, *The Magic Morning*, for a thorough breakdown and guidance on creating a magnificent morning practice (if you haven't read it go get it!).

Suggested morning Practice Activities

- Gratitude List
- Affirmations
- Meditation
- Reading Personal Development
- Exercise
- Deep Breathing Techniques
- Visualization
- Journaling

VISION BOARD

A vision board is an incredible tool for manifesting. Think of it as an art project you're sharing with the Universe. Get a large piece of bristol board or cardboard, a pair of scissors, some glue, and a bunch of magazines (or print off images if you have a color printer available to use) and put an image of everything you desire up on the board! For a full vision board making walkthrough read Manifesting on Purpose, day 7 practice.

A vision board bridges thought into something tangible. It allows us to take what we've imagined and put the image right before us. This helps our minds to accept what we want as real, and available to us. It also helps to be a regular reminder of what we're focused on attracting; after a vision board is made, we place it in a prominent area where we'll see it many times daily.

DELEGATE

Generally, if a person has trouble with the belief and faith aspects of manifesting, they also struggle with trusting other people to do things right. Delegating tasks is an excellent way to work on trust. It also allows you to accomplish more, because more people means more things can be done in the same amount of time. Even better, when you delegate you are setting a vision in to motion to be manifested, so you're going to see things happenings right before your eyes.

I know, I know, it's almost too simple. But delegating can be a breakthrough tool in terms of building your trust and faith, and in actualizing many things you want to have done. You can delegate at work by asking for help with a task, you can delegate at home by asking someone to pick up one of your chores, or if you live alone, get a maid, you can delegate to friends when it comes to planning an activity, the list goes on. It doesn't have to be huge, but every little bit counts.

Your time is valuable, so don't spend it on the tasks that you hate or that bore you, when you could be flourishing and making a real contribution in another area. Sure, someone else's method will be different, it may not be 100% what you'd do, but hey, does it *really* matter? If it's on a less than important task, who cares? Get the help and focus your energy where it's better suited.

- **To-Do List**

  - Incorporate at least 1 of the belief activities above starting today

  - Set a timeline for incorporating the rest into your life

  - Get *Manifesting on Purpose: A 3 Week guide to Transforming Your Life Through the Law of Attraction* to hone in on strengthening your faith in the yet unseen

Chapter 18: Let Go

More than anything you need to believe in yourself and your goals and your ability to achieve it all. Seeking outside approval will always leave you grasping for more and leave a sense of uncertainty when the spotlight isn't on you. When you really go for it, there'll be supporters and naysayers, fans and haters. The thing you need to remember at all times in that only opinion that matters is yours.

I want you to think about your favorite celebrity. A person you absolutely love, their message resonates with your soul, you adore them for everything they do, you think they're brave and bold, and just all around incredible! What they've created and shared with the world has changed your life.

Maybe it's your favorite musician whose songs help you feel better, maybe it's an actor whose brought to life a character you connect with deeply, maybe it's a director that's passionate about sharing a message with the world you love, or an author whose written books that transport you to another realm, or a chef that has introduced you to cooking foods you now don't know how you ever lived without; whatever it is, you freakin' love them for what they've done!

That person who you can't imagine your life without having their awesome influence in it... they have haters! And when they went after their dream, they had naysayers who tried to talk them out of it. Aren't you glad they ignored the naysayers, and continue to ignore the haters, and keep producing their craft for you to enjoy?!

Now it's your turn to go after your dream, and you're going to have to put the naysayers on mute. And when you get your first hater, don't get upset, get excited! You're doing something big and badass enough that it's getting attention; chalk up that first hater to a win at capturing an audience. Remember that for that 1 individual trying to put you down, your inspiring countless others to do amazing things.

CRITICISM VS CONSTRUCTIVE CRITICISM

Constructive criticism is an important and healthy part of personal growth, but criticism for criticisms sake is a big old waste of time for everyone involved. It's important to note, as well, you have to live your life for you, not for your mom, your teacher, your spouse, society, or anyone else. That means even in the ways of constructive criticism, it has to ring true for you. If we listened to, and implemented, every little bit of criticism (good or bad) that we heard into our lives, we'd never ever get anything done.

Criticism

Plain out criticism is when people just basically judge the crap out of what someone else is doing for the sake of I-know-it-all snobbery. It's a waste of everybody's time and accomplishes nothing. These critics need a mute button and a kick is the arse to go pursue their own dreams instead of trying to tear down someone else's.

Constructive Criticism

Constructive criticism can be useful feedback. When someone looks at what we're doing objectively and has advice to offer on how we might improve upon what we're doing, that can be helpful advice. *However*, you know what your dream is supposed to look like, they don't. Maybe you're doing what you're doing for a reason relating to your big picture. In that case, ignore the advice. But on the other hand, perhaps you're in a situation where their fresh perspective sheds light on something you hadn't considered, that makes it a good option to consider what they have said.

The important thing with constructive criticism is to set your ego aside and try to look at your project objectively. I know that can be challenging with the amount of blood, sweat, and tears, that go into bringing your vision to life. The thing is that their advice isn't saying, "You did it wrong," it's saying, "I love it, and here's my idea to contribute to this amazing thing you're doing!"

YOUR OPINION IS THE ONLY ONE THAT MATTERS

Living your best life means the best life *you* envision for you. It's not about trying to fulfill anyone else's vision or expectation about your life. Taking ownership of who you are, and what you want, is the only way to do this.

Walking to the beat of your own drum can feel intimidating at first, especially if you're used to trying to please others. Here's the thing... you can't pour from an empty glass. If you don't feel totally and completely fulfilled, you can't really help anyone else to flourish. It's by taking a big brave step, trusting yourself, and ignoring what anyone else might have to say about it, and just freakin' going for it!

Get some ear plugs so you don't have to hear anyone else's opinion try to sway you.

CONFIDENCE

Self-confidence is vital, in all areas of our lives. Confidence can be built upon, it's as much a skill and a habit as anything. Self-talk is one of the main ways we view ourselves. Developing a positive self-talk, praising ourselves instead of tearing ourselves down, is a habit. We have to train our brains to start embracing the new way of thinking.

Adapting new physical habits can aid as well. Sitting and standing tall, instead of slouching, helps us to feel more confident. One of the best habits to adapt is to stand in superman pose for 30 seconds to 1 minute several times a day. To do this, stand with your feet hip width apart, your hands in fists resting on your hips, arms to your sides, chest forward, and chin up (you know, like a super hero stands!). This pose helps you embody the feeling of confidence. Do this regularly and you'll notice a distinct difference in how you feel about yourself.

BELIEF IN YOURSELF

You know how many of our heroes were told "No," "That's a bad idea," "You're not good enough," etc.? Not just by their family, and friends, and colleagues, but by big important industry people too. A lot of people bow out when they face that kind of rejection, "Ok, sorry to have wasted your time, going back to my day job now..." It's those that believe in themselves, and keep trying, that find their way to success.

- Soichiro Honda had a dream of creating and manufacturing a metal piston ring to sell to Toyota. His prototype was quickly rejected. Soichiro went on to found the Honda Motor Company.

- Bill Gates' first company completely failed and tanked. He went on to create Microsoft and was the richest man alive for years.

- Oprah was fired from her first television job. She didn't let the rejection stop her and went on to be one of the most famous TV personalities of our time, as well as the first female African American billionaire.

- Albert Einstein's teachers thought he was lazy. Einstein went on to become one of the greatest scientist of all time.

- Jeff Bezos had an idea to create an online book store in the 1990's. He told his boss who said, "It would be a better idea for someone who didn't already have a good job." Jeff went on to create Amazon and is now the richest man alive.

- Steven Spielberg was rejected from film school. Twice. He went on to become one of the most incredibly sought-after film makers of our time and household name.

- Vera Wang wanted to be a professional figure skater, but she didn't make the cut for the Olympic team in 1986. She went on to build a fashion empire.

Can you see the thread here? Rejection and failure can't stop you. Other people telling you "no," only matters if you believe it. You have to believe in yourself. No matter what. Because you are freaking amazing, and unstoppable, and you are going to build your dream life!

- **To-Do List**

  - Make a pledge to yourself that you are going to stop caring and giving into other people's opinions about your life

  - Incorporate the confidence building exercises into your daily habits

  - Write down a list of 10 things you are awesome at

Chapter 19:

Hard Work Always Beats Talent

If you have any doubts because you think that you're not naturally amazing at the thing you wish to pursue, now's the time to let go of the idea that that actually matters. If you are naturally talented in the area you want to focus on, don't think for a second that talent alone will be enough for the long haul. Talent can help you get your foot in the door, but it quickly becomes meaningless in the face of ongoing work and adaptability in the face of changes.

Example:

An actor that's always had a natural knack to step into a character's shoes. They have a lot of fun on stage and are great at engaging an audience. If that actor rests on that talent alone, they'll never progress to be able to take on more challenging roles.

Another actor, who doesn't have the natural charisma, but is determined to learn, will take classes, hire an acting coach, practice in front of a camera and watch their own performance to learn from it countless times. They will continue to perfect their skill until they surpass that of that naturally gifted actor.

CONSISTENCY

What does matter? Consistency. That boils down to the daily habits you set yourself up for. It's the small things we do daily that add up to massive change over time. Think about the incredible power water has to erode stone over time. It's the everyday things that matter.

DEVELOPING SUCCESSFUL HABITS

We're naturally inclined to develop habits and routines. Many of the things we do in a given day are automatic habits we've formed over the years; these are activities we do without even having to think about them. This makes it incredible easy to embrace new habits into our lives.

How do we add a new habit? We make the decision to incorporate it. It takes 21 days of consecutive behavior for a new habit to become automatic, however after just a few days it will become anticipated. One of the best things you can do while forming a new habit is to schedule it into your daily planner. If you don't use a daily planner, put it into your reminders and notifications.

What habits should you adapt? Certain specific habits will depend on what you're looking to accomplish. Take a look at successful people who have done what you'd like to accomplish and adapt their habits.

There are also some Universal habits that successful people do that all of us should adapt...

Some Helpful Universal Habits to Adapt:

- Daily Exercise
- Drink a minimum of half your body weight (pounds) in water daily (ounces). Example: 150-pound person would drink minimum 75oz water
- Daily Meditation
- Daily Gratitude Practice
- Do the thing you *least* look forward to first
- Create a morning routine and don't veer from it
- Don't use any tech within the first hour of waking (no phone, e-mail, internet)
- Incorporate Daily Personal Development

GETTING RID OF BAD HABITS

How do you get rid of a bad habit? First you decide it's no longer part of your life, for good. *Goodbye, adios, see ya never!* Second, replace it with a good habit. This second part is just as crucial as the first, and one that many people don't implement.

When you say, "I'm not going to _____ anymore," then you need a plan for what to do when you'd normally do that habit. It's called a habit because it's become a daily part of our routine, and we feel incredibly out of sorts when that gets interrupted. You need a replacement activity. Ideally the replacement will engage mind and body, which provides a full distraction. Just as it takes 21 days to make a habit, it takes 21 days to break one, so stick to your decision. There is no going back, you burned the bridge, and you will move forward to better things.

Your habits will be the solid foundation that creates massive change over time.

OUTWORK THE COMPETITION

No matter what someone else is doing, you can outwork them. Dedication, and discipline, trump talent. A body builder may have a naturally muscular body, but another dedicated person could outwork them and win the competition. An employee may naturally be excellent at a certain task, but another determined employee could outwork them and surpass them. Mindset is everything. It's the person who does whatever it takes to succeed that stands at the top.

- **To-Do List**
    - Make a pledge to yourself to adapt all of the Universal successful habits
    - Add 1 new habit this week to accomplish something you've been putting off
    - Replace 1 bad habit with a new good habit this week

Chapter 20: Growth

Consistent personal growth is the key to living your best life. That which does not adapt to change, dies. This can seem scary to some, but when you realize constant growth and change means a whole stream of new amazing experiences happening regularly, it becomes a joyous way to live!

When we stop pushing and challenging ourselves and get stuck in a rut of automatic patterns of behavior, we end up feeling bitter resentment and jealousy towards those that are living large and in charge. When we're stagnant, we're not happy. Growth is a natural part of our existence.

There's something about familiarity, living in our comfort zone, that draws us into the illusion that we're just fine with where we're at now, so we don't have to deal with change. But here's the rub... that's an illusion. There's no control, you can't pause time, there's no keeping things exactly as they are. Either you grow with change, or you get left behind.

COMOFRT ZONES ARE UNCOMFORTABLE

The comfort zone illusion is that "new is scary," so it's more comfortable to stay where we're at. But, who the hell are we fooling? It's not comfortable at all to stay where we're at! Our deep-rooted longing to experience new things and become the best version of us is screaming for us to take action!

DO SOMETHING THAT SCARES YOU

What have you been putting off? What's something you'd love to do, but it's intimidating, and so you haven't tried doing it yet? Maybe it's work related, maybe it's personal, but when you think of it you get excited, followed by terrified?

- Travelling abroad
- Starting your own business
- Learning to do some sort of tech thing that's over your head
- Making a sales call
- Asking someone you have a crush on out on a date
- Skydiving
- Learning how to drive

- Swimming in the ocean

- Quitting the job you hate

- Investing in the stock market

- Buying something really expensive

- Riding a rollercoaster

- Learning about managing your finances

- Going back to school

- Public speaking

- Saying "hi," to a complete stranger

- Taking on the leadership role

- Setting up a job interview for the position you've always wanted

- Getting a tattoo

- Rock climbing

- Learn a new language

This list could be infinite. We all have some hang up somewhere that someone else doesn't even bat an eye at doing. So, what's that for you? Regularly push yourself to do something that's scary, and suddenly your list of fears shrinks smaller and smaller. Fear is in our minds, and once we conquer the challenge, it's no longer intimidating. Go. Do. IT!

GET COMFORTABLE BEING UNCOMFORTABLE

When you're in a state of constant growth, you will always be expanding the size of your comfort zone. When you can get used to that feeling of always pushing your boundaries, that beautiful fear-excitement, and embrace it, you become unstoppable. You never want to stop growing, so it's absolutely key that you get comfortable being uncomfortable.

Ways to Keep Expanding your Comfort Zone:

- Always be learning something new
- If it scares you, you should probably do it
- Take action when opportunities strike
- Make a list of things you've always wanted to do, and one by one make it happen
- Have your success partner and/or coach throw challenges your way
- If you're feeling complacent, it's time to pursue something new

Take stock daily on how you're feeling and your progress towards making things happen. If you're on the edge of your seat, excited beyond belief each day, you're on track. If you're stuck in the same-old routine, shake things up. Keep

growing, learning, and expanding your comfort zone!

- **To-Do List**
    - Choose something to do that you've been too scared to do and DO IT!
    - Make a pledge to yourself to continuously expand the boundaries of your comfort zone

Chapter 21: Never Give Up

If there's one bit of advice worth taking to heart, it's to never give up. Tenacity is what separates success from failure. True failure only happens when you throw in the towel, so get used to picking that towel up after you tumble, wipe your face, and get back in the game!

You're at the wheel, and you're steering the direction your life is going. You choose what road you're taking. It's never a straight path, there's bumps along the way, and a helluva-lot of sightseeing. Your car might stall, or even break down along the way. That's just part of the trip. Get that sucker fixed up and keep on truckin' down that road. The only way to get to your ultimate destination is to never stop heading in the direction you need to go to get there.

YOUR 'WHY'

The most important thing you need to know when you're embarking on a massive life-changing journey is your *reason why*. If you're just doing it because, "I think it'll be fun," or you haven't taken the time to really dig deep into your own motivations, you'll quit when it gets hard. So, be really honest with yourself here, why do you want what you're working towards?

No one can answer this for you. It may take some soul-searching to figure it out. It may also lead you to realize you're trying to live out someone else's idea of what's best for you. That's never an easy realization but it allows you to release the need to please them and determine what it is that *you* truly want.

Perhaps it's been a life-long dream or will enable you the freedom to live a certain lifestyle you desire or will give you the means to make in impact in other's lives that leaves you feeling fulfilled. Does it light your heart up? Why?

Example:

I want to be a stand-up comic because it is a lot of fun for me to do it. It brings me joy when other people laugh. I've always wanted to bring a more positive vibe to life and I feel that laugher is the means to that end. I was always scared to do this because it isn't a 'safe' career, but I know I'm capable, and talented, and have what it takes. I have to do this for me, because my soul-sucking 9 to 5 job is no longer an option. I'm doing this to be happy! I deserve happiness!

HOW TO STAY THE COURSE WHEN THE GOING GETS TOUGH

First of all, the going will get tough. It just will. When you're making major shifts in your life, you'll face new challenges, that's just part of the process. So, fair warning here, so you should be completely prepared when it happens. No feigning surprise after this because you now know to expect it.

Your 'why' is your motivation when the going gets tough. When you feel like giving up you have to remember why you started. We are leaving our old limp-noodle lives behind for a reason: we weren't thrilled with how our lives were! You don't want to go back to that.

Grab a set of sticky notes and write down your 'why' in little fragments.

Using the example above:

- *I deserve Happiness*
- *I'm doing this to be happy!*
- *My 9-to-5 job was soul-sucking and I will not go back!*

- *I want to create positivity on this planet*
- *I love to make people laugh*
- *I believe in me*
- *I am capable*
- *I am a stand-up comic!*

You could write more than this; the key here is to capture the essence and the power phrases that make you feel totally empowered. Put these up in a place where you're going to see them multiple times daily. You want a constant reminder. You're also going to add in your #1 statement from your 'why' into your phone that pops up as a reminder at least 3 times a day.

Whenever you hit a road bump or have an overwhelming bad day, you're going to remind yourself of your why. It's going to keep your fire fanned, so you don't let the passion you have burn out. Your 'why' is your lifeline; keep it close at all times.

Remember that the road to living your best life is full of challenges, and through those challenges we grow into who we need to become to fully appreciate that life and be the person we need to be.

- **To-Do List**

- Write out your why
- Write out bite-sized segments of your why onto sticky notes to put up somewhere you'll see the multiple times a day
- Add you #1 segment of your why into your phone as a daily reminder that pops up at least 3 times
- Remember your 'why' is your lifeline to keep you afloat when things get tough

If you never give up, you cannot fail.

ABOUT THE AUTHOR

Amanda Rose, author of Manifesting on Purpose, Fire Fury Freedom, The Impending End, and A Strange Dream: An Anthology of Short Stories and Poems, is an avid reader and storyteller. Working in a variety of mediums and genres, communicating new ways of thinking is her passion.

Amanda works as an online Health and Fitness coach, Law of Attraction Coach, Actor, Model, and Writer. Residing in Kingston, Ontario, with her husband and 3 cats, Amanda is currently working on her next novel.

Get in touch with Amanda by visiting her website: www.AmandaRoseFitness.com

Made in the USA
San Bernardino, CA
13 May 2020